LawExpress
JURISPRUDENCE

Tried and tested

Law Express has been helping UK law students to revise since 2009 and its power is proven. A recent survey[*] shows that:

- **94%** think that Law Express helps them to revise effectively and take exams with confidence.
- **88%** agree Law Express helps them to understand key concepts quickly.

Individual students attest to how the series has supported their revision:

'Law Express are my go-to guides. They are an excellent supplement to my course material.'

Claire Turner, Open University

'In the modules in which I used these books to revise, generally the modules I found the most difficult, I got the highest marks. The books are really easy to use and are extremely helpful.'

Charlotte Evans, Queen Mary University of London

'The information is straight to the point. This is important particularly for exams.'

Dewan Sadia Kuraishy, University of Manchester

'These revision guides strike the right balance between enough detail to help shape a really good answer, but brief enough to be used for last-minute revision. The layout is user friendly and the use of tables and flowcharts is helpful.'

Shannon Reynolds, University of Manchester

'I personally found the series very helpful in my preparation for exams.'

Abba Elgujja, University of Salford

[*] A survey of 16 UK law students in September 2014.

JURISPRUDENCE

Law Express

2nd edition

Julia J. A. Shaw
Reader in Law and Literary Jurisprudence
De Montfort University, Leicester
School of Law

PEARSON

Harlow, England • London • New York • Boston • San Francisco • Toronto • Sydney • Auckland • Singapore • Hong Kong
Tokyo • Seoul • Taipei • New Delhi • Cape Town • São Paulo • Mexico City • Madrid • Amsterdam • Munich • Paris • Milan

Pearson Education Limited
Edinburgh Gate
Harlow CM20 2JE
United Kingdom
Tel: +44 (0)1279 623623
Web: www.pearson.com/uk

First published 2014 (print and electronic)
Second edition published 2017 (print and electronic)

© Pearson Education Limited 2014, 2017 (print and electronic)

ISBN: 978-1-292-08693-4 (print)
       978-1-292-08710-8 (PDF)
       978-1-292-08709-2 (ePub)

British Library Cataloguing-in-Publication Data
A catalogue record for the print edition is available from the British Library

10 9 8 7 6 5 4 3 2
20 19 18 17

Front cover bestseller data from Nielsen BookScan (2009–2014, Law Revision Series).
Back cover poll data from a survey of 16 UK law students in September 2014.

Print edition typeset in 10/12 pts Helvetica Neue LT W1G by Lumina Datamatics
Print edition printed and bound in Malaysia (CTP-PJB)

NOTE THAT ANY PAGE CROSS REFERENCES REFER TO THE PRINT EDITION

Contents

What do you think of LawExpress?

We're really keen to hear your opinions about the series and how well it supports your studies. Your views will help inform the future development of Law Express and ensure it is best suited to the revision needs of law students.

Please log on to the website and leave us your feedback. It will only take a few minutes and your thoughts are invaluable to us.

www.pearsoned.co.uk/lawexpressfeedback

Acknowledgements

I would like to acknowledge, first and foremost, my undergraduate law tutors, Costas Douzinas, Peter Goodrich and Ronnie Warrington, for illuminating the oft-hidden realm of law's language, fictions, myths and emblems – and whose 'critical thinking' teaching style inspired a lifelong love of literary jurisprudence and the philosophy of law. Many thanks to Donna Goddard and Christine Statham for their welcome advice and guidance at all stages in preparing the original manuscript, and to the reviewers and my own students, whose invaluable feedback contributed to the final content and rhetorical style of particular topics. For the provision of useful suggestions, constructive criticism and general support, my heartfelt appreciation to Hillary Shaw without whom life would be a lot less interesting.

Julia J.A. Shaw

Publisher's acknowledgements

Our thanks go to all reviewers who contributed to the development of this text, including students who participated in research and focus groups that helped to shape the series format.

Introduction

Jurisprudence is a popular option at many universities, and a compulsory module at others. Modules with the same or very similar content are sometimes referred to as 'legal theory' or the 'philosophy of law'. Unlike a traditional legal subject such as contract or land law, which will define, categorise and impose conditions as relevant to that particular field of study, jurisprudence is not simply a matter of becoming familiar with another bounded legal topic. It rests on the assumption that the foundations of legal knowledge are not fixed; rather, laws are contingent and so constitute the proper object of inquiry as to their underlying motivations and justifications. This means that by studying jurisprudence you will acquire a generic and profound critical understanding of the law, which rests on an interdisciplinary approach to fundamental questions about law and (real or ideal) legal systems. Scrutiny of primary sources within jurisprudence will encourage further development of the legal vocabulary, demystify theoretical legal language and enhance the critical facilities by learning how to approach and critically reflect on primary texts in legal philosophy. You will develop the ability to make connections between different theorists and theories, to articulate new insights and evaluate their practical doctrinal implications.

This jurisprudence revision guide introduces the theoretical bases of law as distinct from, yet still relevant to, legal practice. The same legal concepts and issues are addressed; however, legal theorists discuss these in a more general and critical manner. By examining the same subject matter as the black letter tradition, only by using different philosophical spectacles, it is possible to gain a deeper understanding of the nature of law, legal reasoning, legal concepts and legal institutions. Jurisprudence addresses questions arising from the advancement of doctrinal law, such as: What is law and why does it matter?; Are there unjust laws?; How much law is really necessary?; What are the appropriate limits and justifications for law?; What is the relationship between law, morality and justice?; Do judges make law or do they find it?; Does law in effect do something other than what it purports to do?; and What considerations determine one legal argument as making more sense than another? These are just a small sample of questions that form the starting point for much inquiry and debate. A range of diverse disciplines such as philosophy, sociology, economics, history, literature and psychology are used in investigating the legitimacy and appropriateness of key legal doctrines. This multidisciplinary approach, evident from the writing of key legal theorists, seeks to provide a comprehensive account of the complex interrelationships between law, society and the individual as well as the broader role law is required to play in modern politics and society.

Since there is some variation between different university syllabuses in this subject, the revision guide seeks to provide the widest possible overview of a comprehensive range of topics that may be encountered at any law school. Wherever it is studied, many students tend initially to struggle with the complex terminology, the argumentative attitude of jurisprudence and, in particular, the larger proportion of theoretical material. Grand themes, such as law and morality, rights and justice are covered, as well as traditional approaches such as natural law and legal positivism, alongside the more modern branches, critical legal studies and sociological jurisprudence. Under each heading there is an introduction to, and explanation of, a diverse range of sub-topics, central issues and key terms. Although not a substitute for reading original essays by key jurists or other primary sources, this study companion signposts in brief and simple terms the main areas, ideas and approaches that characterise the subject. It will help you to quickly grasp abstract terminology, the main themes of key theories and key issues, so you have the foundational knowledge from which to elaborate a well-constructed and coherent essay or examination answer.

Within the legal profession and wider society, employers are increasingly looking for graduates with the ability to do more than demonstrate bare technical ability; jurisprudence is capable of providing students with an impressive range of advanced analytical skills and critical legal insight. This guide provides the basic building blocks from which to begin asking the 'What is law?' question, along with advice on how to challenge the views of key jurists and cultivate a speculative frame of mind in your reading and research.

> ### 📖 REVISION NOTE
>
> - This revision guide will assist you in mapping the key topics in jurisprudence. Be aware of the many connections and relationships between alternative theories, theorists and issues.
>
> - Demonstrate your understanding of a variety of different perspectives, by providing a rich, well-supported, comparative analysis of differing approaches to a particular issue.
>
> - Jurisprudence is an argumentative area of legal study. Whether you agree or disagree with a particular theorist does not negate the significance of their perspective; your analysis should at all times be objective.
>
> - Use this revision text as a guide to approaching core themes within jurisprudence, legal theory and/or the philosophy of law. Do not be tempted to rely on it as a comprehensive guide to everything there is to know about the subject for essay or examination purposes.
>
> - Jurisprudence utilises many important, although initially less familiar, words, ideas and concepts. Enjoy enlarging your knowledge base and vocabulary by looking up and learning these new words and concepts. This will ensure your well-researched writing shows a high level of articulacy, and will greatly enhance your overall legal advocacy skills.
>
> **Before you begin, you can use the study plan available on the companion website to assess how well you know the material in this book and identify the areas where you may want to focus your revision.**

Guided tour

How to use features in the book 📖 and on the companion website 🖱️

Understand quickly

📖 **Topic maps** – Visual guides highlight key subject areas and facilitate easy navigation through the chapter. Download them from the companion website to pin on your wall or add to your revision notes.

📖 **Key definitions** – Make sure you understand essential legal terms.

📖 **Key cases and key statutes** – Identify and review the important elements of essential cases and statutes you will need to know for your exams.

📖 **Read to impress** – These carefully selected sources will extend your knowledge, deepen your understanding, and earn better marks in coursework and exams.

📖 **Glossary** – Forgotten the meaning of a word? This quick reference covers key definitions and other useful terms.

🖱️ **Test your knowledge** – How well do you know each topic? Test yourself with quizzes tailored specifically to each chapter.

🖱️ **Podcasts** – Listen as your own personal Law Express tutor guides you through a step-by-step explanation of how to approach a typical but challenging question.

Revise effectively

📖 **Revision checklists** – Identify essential points you should know for your exams. The chapters will help you revise each point to ensure you are fully prepared. Print the checklists from the companion website to track your progress.

📖 **Revision notes** – These boxes highlight related points and areas where your course might adopt a particular approach that you should check with your course tutor.

Study plan – Assess how well you know a subject prior to your revision and determine which areas need the most attention. Take the full assessment or focus on targeted study units.

Flashcards – Test and improve recall of important legal terms, key cases and statutes. Available in both electronic and printable formats.

Take exams with confidence

Sample questions with answer guidelines – Practice makes perfect! Consider how you would answer the question at the start of each chapter then refer to answer guidance at the end of the chapter. Try out additional sample questions online.

Assessment advice – Use this feature to identify how a subject may be examined and how to apply your knowledge effectively.

Make your answer stand out – Impress your examiners with these sources of further thinking and debate.

Exam tips – Feeling the pressure? These boxes indicate how you can improve your exam performance when it really counts.

Don't be tempted to – Spot common pitfalls and avoid losing marks.

You be the marker – Evaluate sample exam answers and understand how and why an examiner awards marks.

The nature and scope of jurisprudence

Revision checklist

Essential points you should know:

- [ ] The nature and scope of jurisprudence: asking the 'What is the law?' question
- [ ] The etymology of jurisprudence
- [ ] Four common approaches to jurisprudential inquiry
- [ ] The main schools of jurisprudence and their key characteristics
- [ ] The language and vocabulary of jurisprudence

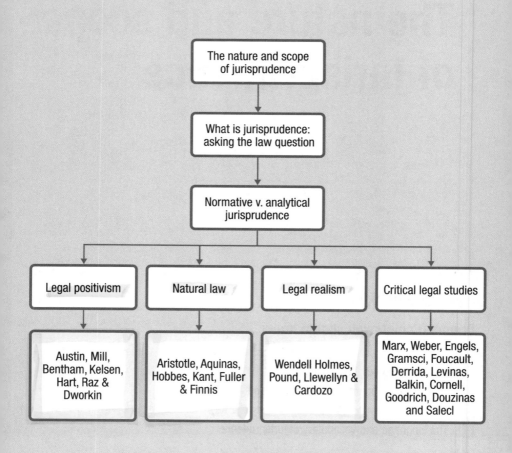

A printable version of this topic map is available from www.pearsoned.co.uk/lawexpress

Introduction

'Law, says the judge as he looks down his nose; Law is, as you know, I suppose; Law is, but let me explain it once more; "Law is The Law" is the law'.

This is a slightly amended version of a famous poem by W.H. Auden called 'Law like Love'. In it Auden suggests that, like love and the vows made by lovers, man-made law is arbitrary, capricious and its promises are 'seldom kept'. It cannot always protect the vulnerable, and is often disappointing and confusing; which prompts us to ask 'what is law?'. This leads to a further question, namely, what 'ought' the law to be? This is the point at which we can appreciate the relevance of jurisprudence. Unlike 'black letter' law, which focuses on the technical nature of law, the study of jurisprudence views the origins and evolution of legal doctrine as belonging to a distinctive philosophy of legal thought, each with its own characteristics and content. Important foundational legal concepts such as right, duty, justice, ownership and liberty are explicated from within a variety of diverse jurisprudential schools. By examining the same subject matter as the black letter tradition, only by using different philosophical spectacles, scholars of jurisprudence hope to gain a deeper understanding of the nature of law, legal reasoning, legal concepts and legal institutions.

The concerns of jurisprudence are much the same as those that arise in both a legal context and from within wider society, which means there is an inherent connection between the law and the social sciences. Since legal concepts are formulated by, and imposed upon, particular communities of people (those who make the law and those who are subject to, and objects of, the law), the arts and humanities also relate to law. History and language, for example, are important since law's legitimacy rests on the transmission of its ancient traditions, and relies on both the text (cases and statutes) and image (visual metaphors, court etiquette and forms of dress) from which it derives its identity and authority. Just remember that although jurisprudence is considered to be a difficult subject area, by acquiring a philosophical understanding of some of the most commonly used legal principles, you will better understand the nature, function, purpose and possibilities of law. This also means you will become a better law student, legal scholar or practising lawyer.

ASSESSMENT ADVICE

An essay question is likely to ask you to outline the main schools of jurisprudence or to perform a comparative analysis using only two or three. You need to be familiar with the main characteristics of each legal philosophy and be prepared to illustrate these by using examples of key legal theorists in each case. Their opinions on various themes, such as right, duty, justice and fairness demonstrate the points of departure, conflict and consensus in each case. Gaining an understanding of the unique features of each school of thought will enable you to write an essay that recognises the development of law as and dependent upon certain considerations – for example, economic, social, historical and political. A good answer will demonstrate an awareness of the main jurisprudential schools along with key legal theorists, and their responses to an important doctrinal issue such as the relationship of law and morality or concepts such as duty, right and ownership.

◼ Sample question

Could you answer this question? Below is a typical essay question that could arise on this topic. Guidelines on answering the question are included at the end of this chapter. Another sample question and guidance on tackling it can be found on the companion website.

ESSAY QUESTION

Dworkin claimed in *Law's Empire* that since there are no immutable criteria for decision-making, 'jurisprudence is the general part of adjudication, silent prologue to any decision of law'. Do you agree that it is necessary to engage with legal philosophy/theories of law, in order to discover what the law is? Discuss.

◼ The etymology of jurisprudence

It is a good idea to understand the origins and historical development (or etymology) of words as they can give us a good indication of the original purpose and essence of a particular subject. Originating from the Roman Senate, **jurisprudence** has been referred to as the 'queen of reason' and 'a gladsome light' by Sir Edward Coke in 1628 and, by Blackstone quoting Aristotle in 1809, as 'the principal and most perfect branch of ethics'. These jurists and philosophers were insinuating that ethical principles arise out of human practice, not from the abstract formulation of universal rules that claim to apply to all human conditions at all times. Famous philosopher and economist Adam Smith provided a narrower definition, stating 'jurisprudence is the theory of rules by which governments ought to be directed'. The precise meaning of the term 'jurisprudence' has evolved since Roman times and today there are many definitions of jurisprudence. It is clear from such examples, however, that jurisprudence can set limits for law, and provide justification for its means by being aware of its ends (in other words, the likely consequences of a specific course of action).

KEY DEFINITION: Jurisprudence

Jurisprudence is described as the philosophy or theory of law. Historically, it derives from the late Latin term *juris prudentia*, which means the study, knowledge or science of the law.

The significance of jurisprudence along with the aims and objectives of modern jurisprudential inquiry are essentially the same as those of earlier times. Just as the word *prudentia* translates from Latin to English as 'prudence', good sense or wisdom, it could be argued that without jurisprudence there is no wisdom in law; furthermore, without jurisprudential inquiry there is no legitimate authority, only our own arbitrary desires.

Be critical

Argument is a key characteristic of jurisprudence; as it encompasses a diverse range of contrasting theories and ideas. This means it is necessary to adopt a critical approach to the subject. You need to remember that unlike other disciplines or legal subjects, which produce classifications enabling the strict identification of certain typical behaviours and appearances, jurisprudence is different. The various jurisprudential schools do not purport to set clear limits between each category; even the nature and number of these categories is often disputed. The amount of conflicting opinion, shifting perspectives and multitudinous interpretations produced with the passage of time may seem confusing.

Your tutor may present jurisprudence according to the content of key legal theories and theorists, which is a historical method based on comparing key bodies of thought and their points of disagreement. Alternatively, jurisprudence may be taught on the basis of issues – for example, discussing the possible legalisation of human cloning by reference to legal theories that discuss key aspects of such a debate. Either way, there is no right or wrong way to 'do' jurisprudence.

▓ Four common approaches to jurisprudence

The role of jurisprudence is similar to the function of the engineer who designs a particular model of car or the architect who draws up the plans for a house. Each provides a comprehensive framework for mapping the necessary components and materials, how these will work together, and ensures optimal levels of maintenance and performance. It is therefore the architect and design engineer who have conceived the possibility of a beautiful house or a sports car, and not those who assemble the car or build the house. Similarly, jurisprudence provides the theory of law that acts as a foundation for understanding legal materials as being developed from a set of legal principles, which are themselves contingent upon social phenomena and other considerations. Jurisprudence therefore attempts to offer a common perspective on the nature of law and seeks to find some unifying explanation or theory. These four approaches provide a rough guide to the main purposes of jurisprudential inquiry – in other words, what kind of questions and answers jurisprudence demands from the law in order that it may justify its legitimacy (or rightful authority) in assuming or performing particular functions, and in relation to specific issues.

As legal, moral and political philosopher Joseph Raz explains in his 1994 *Ethics in the Public Domain* that any useful theory of society is based on 'evaluative considerations in that its success is in highlighting important social structures and processes, and every judgment of importance is evaluative and every good judgement is evaluative'. Jurisprudence uses an evaluative **methodology**, in that it is critical and seeks to appraise and consider by weighing up and judging carefully those factors that construct, confound and often complicate our various understandings of law, its nature, use and purpose. There are four broad objectives of jurisprudential inquiry and these can be summarised as:

■ to expose the historical, moral and cultural foundations of a particular legal concept or principle;
■ to compare and contrast law with other disciplines such as the social sciences, politics, economics and literature;
■ to discover the answer to 'big' questions relating to the purpose of law, appropriate modes of adjudication and the legitimate scope of legal authority;
■ to explain, categorise and critically analyse the entire *corpus juris*; which is the purpose of most jurisprudence textbooks.

 Make your answer stand out

When considering your answer to a general question concerning the significance of jurisprudence and why jurisprudence is still relevant to modern lawyering and legal scholarship, you will be able to give examples of how it examines those factors (external to law) that influence the decisions of law-makers. For example, the judiciary may be influenced by cultural and theological considerations in their determination of key legal concepts, relating to such controversial areas as euthanasia or abortion.

■ Normative v. analytical jurisprudence

In simple terms, it has been said that the purpose of law is to organise, even coerce, human behaviour and constitute a form of social organisation whereby its legal agents are able to apply sanctions to ensure conformity with the law and its principles. In order for this exercise of control over individuals in society to be legitimate, it has to accord with certain ethical standards and safeguards put in place by, and guaranteed by, legal authority. Legal authority is derived from legal principle, which itself originates from (1) legal theory or (2) philosophy of law or (3) jurisprudence. Generally speaking, these three terms are the same and used interchangeably, and they all indicate those concepts and schools of thought that are necessary to understanding the nature of law, as well as all aspects of legal rules and legal systems – and in particular how these relate to society. Two mainstream categories of philosophical thought are **normative jurisprudence** and **analytical jurisprudence**.

> **KEY DEFINITION: Normative jurisprudence**
>
> The starting point of normative jurisprudence is the already established concept of law and so, having understood what the law *is*, it aims to understand the moral basis for the law. In other words, it is concerned with what the law *ought* to be. It seeks to provide a theory that determines what is morally right and just and is, therefore, concerned about the criteria by which the law should be evaluated.

Normative jurisprudence asks questions that relate to law and freedom, such as the conditions for the possibility of freedom of expression. The proper role and justification of punishment and the moral limits of criminal law, the relationship between law and morality and the enforcement of morality are other common topics for consideration. By contrast, analytical jurisprudence is concerned with the formal question of, for example, 'what is a right?' and 'what does it mean to have a right to something?'; whereas normative jurisprudence seeks to determine the moral foundation of rights and examines 'what rights do we actually have?' or 'ought to have'.

> **KEY DEFINITION: Analytical jurisprudence**
>
> Analytical (or sometimes referred to as 'analytic') jurisprudence has been described, by John Austin, as the study of the nature of law only at its most general and abstract level. Although its boundaries are not clearly defined, it is concerned with the formal analysis of concepts and seeks to analyse law and legal constructs from a neutral viewpoint, according to the key facets. Analytical theory asks such questions as 'what *is* the law?' and 'what is the relationship between law and morality?' at a descriptive level.

Unlike normative jurisprudence, analytical jurisprudence only seeks to describe such phenomena, the terms of their existence and nature of their relationships – even though it asks some of the same questions. The purpose is to reveal the logical structure of legal concepts in order to refine conceptual differences. The scope of inquiry is dissimilar from normative jurisprudence; it looks for different answers – descriptive rather than prescriptive – in other words, what is the law, rather than what should the law be.

Clearly, there is some scope for overlap between these two as they are closely related. Critical legal studies and outsider jurisprudence offers a more recently conceived third perspective, comprising multiple topics and, for example, issues affecting so-called minority interests and underrepresented social groups.

■ Main schools of jurisprudence

There are a number of schools of jurisprudential inquiry, and below is a brief introduction to four main schools of jurisprudence. These, and others, are covered in greater depth in the following chapters under their respective headings.

Natural law

Natural law deals with the question of what are valid legal rules or sources of law, and is based on the idea that the sources of law include a *moral* test of validity. Human reason, philosophy, conscience and theology, for example, are also valid and often argued to be a more appropriate source of rightful authority. Classical natural legal theorists such as Aquinas, and modern natural lawyers such as John Finnis, have appealed to a higher authority of law that, because it is determined by reason, is capable of producing just and fair laws that have moral authority. Only such laws emanating from 'reason' or human nature, as natural laws, are understood to be just and so worthy of our obedience.

Legal positivism

Classical legal positivists have claimed there is no connection between law and morality, and that rules enacted by governments or law courts are the only legitimate source of legal authority. Modern legal positivists, such as Joseph Raz, have agreed that there is often a link between law and morality but believe it is unnecessary to resort to moral arguments to discover the law. They suggest that, by applying ordinary legal investigatory skills – for example, by analysing judicial decisions and statute, and by explicating social facts, it is possible to determine law's existence and content, although positivists do not agree on what those facts are.

Legal realism

Legal realists argue that only the real-world legal practices of the judiciary influence the development of law, as the judges determine the content of legal rights and duties according to public policy and the prevailing social interests of wider society. Rather than by compliance with abstract legal rules, judicial decision-making is often guided by their intuitions and any moral, political, economic and cultural prejudices.

Critical legal studies

Critical legal studies maintains that law is political, and challenges established legal norms and principles, claiming these result from the policy goals of society's power elites and comprise a set of prejudices with which to legitimise injustice. This theory of jurisprudence incorporates a diverse range of subgroups, such as feminist legal theory, queer theory, critical race theory and **postmodernism**, and relates to other forms of 'outsider jurisprudence'.

⌂ REVISION NOTE

Although some of the names of key legal theorists (for example, Hart, Finnis, Aquinas, Kant, Kelsen, Rawls, Fuller and Dworkin) will be initially unfamiliar, it is important that you are able to place the main ideas and concepts associated with each famous author within the corresponding school of jurisprudential thought.

Be critical

Jurisprudence draws on an immense range of texts, commentary and fundamental disagreement that are subject to constant question and debate. The various legal theories are broadly defined with no clear boundaries; in fact, most theories overlap and borrow from others. The same is true of legal theorists who, in explaining their philosophy, may incorporate traces of other theories. This is because a combination of approaches is often required in addressing the important questions about law. Legal categories are, however, useful in providing a general outline of the different jurisprudential schools, but you should remember that these definitions are imprecise and often contested. Jurisprudence is all about critique, asking questions about law's nature, intentions and rightful goals.

■ The vocabulary of jurisprudence

Unlike other branches of law that rely on cases and statute since they deal with facts and related principles, jurisprudence is based on ideas. These ideas are grounded in a number of intellectual propositions that are based in theory – competing abstract theories – which rely heavily on the use of complex terms that are sometimes capable of multiple meanings. Even though this claim seems to echo Humpty Dumpty's 'a word means anything you want it to mean' and lead to ambiguity and confusion, this is not the case. It means that words can be interpreted as having a significance beyond their dictionary definition or contain properties in addition to those inferred, and at a distinctive level of specificity.

 Make your answer stand out

In jurisprudence, words and the text (also the imagery and possibilities of signification) of law are all very important. It is necessary, therefore, to embrace the process of extending your vocabulary, and learn to apply these slightly altered and recast terms of reference with precision. In this way you will greatly enhance your arguments and demonstrate your understanding of significant concepts.

The legal tradition uses language as its working medium and as a means of organising and evaluating the randomness of human experience; words are chosen deliberately in order to evoke the right images and insinuations. For example, John Rawls refers to justice as fairness; this proposition carries a complex set of relational ideas; these relate to asking 'what is justice?', 'what are the proper objectives of justice?' and 'what is the meaning of fairness?' in a particular context. He goes on to use the metaphor of a 'veil of ignorance', or law's blindfold, behind which all persons are equal and can only be treated irrespective of their observable differences. If you think carefully about these words, they comprise very powerful metaphors; for example, the 'veil of ignorance' lends the word 'ignorance' a positive connotation. The terms 'democracy', 'right' and 'rule' can similarly be explicated according to a particular jurisprudential theory, or frame of reference, which will give them a different set of characteristics and obligations. Of course, 'obligation' is another term that can mean different things from within the context of an alternative legal theory.

📖 REVISION NOTE

Since jurisprudence is a subject where two seemingly contradictory answers can both get excellent marks, it is important that you take the opportunity to discuss what *you* think as often as possible, whether in a seminar class or tutorial, or simply among your fellow students whilst studying or revising. By regularly sharing ideas from your own reading and understanding of main theories and issues, as well as engaging with alternative views, you may be better able to identify key areas of contrast that will help to further develop your own critical abilities.

Jurisprudence uses a range of terms that indicate a distinct approach to its own project. For example, interpreting legal texts has historically been at the heart of legal thought, and the term *hermeneutic* refers to the art or science of interpretation. Certain theories of law are referred to as falling within the hermeneutic tradition of law – for example, those by Friedrich Karl von Savigny, Ronald Dworkin and Peter Goodrich. You may come across the term *dialectical*. The **dialectical** method enables the evaluation, or weighing up, of contradictory facts and theories. Hegel is often associated with this method of arriving at the truth by proposing a thesis, developing a contradictory thesis known as an antithesis, then resolving and bringing them together into a coherent synthesis.

Semiotics is a term that refers to the study of signs, sign-processes and symbols, often associated with the writings of Ferdinand de Saussure. Within critical legal studies, legal scholars work within the tradition of legal **semiotics** because they claim law can be understood as a system of signs and signifiers. This is evident in its institutions, rituals, language and literature. *Moral relativism* is another term you may come across. It refers to the idea that there is no settled, absolute moral law that applies to all people, for all time and in all places; it means that there are many different viewpoints as to what is considered to be moral. As Friedrich Nietzsche wrote, 'You have your way, I have my way. As for the right way, it does not exist.' The European Convention of Human Rights is opposed to **moral relativism** of any kind since it purports to set out a comprehensive catalogue of rights that must apply to all signatory legal jurisdictions and their citizens, irrespective of cultural, religious, social or political differences.

❗ Don't be tempted to . . .

It is important to bear in mind that there are a number of approaches to learning the landscape and language of jurisprudence. You do not have to be familiar with every single approach and their particular nuances, only those themes and methodologies indicated by your tutor and module reading lists. Also, don't panic if you feel you haven't grasped a particular theory, theorist or all aspects of a particular issue. Jurisprudence is one of the more challenging areas of legal study, and certain textbooks and secondary sources are easier to read than others. You need to spend some time in a bookshop or the library to find a text that discusses the same themes in a more accessible fashion.

■ Putting it all together

Answer guidelines

See the sample question at the start of the chapter.

Approaching the question

Your first task is to make sense of the quotation in relation to what the essay is asking you to do. This requires understanding any unfamiliar words or expressions. In this case, you may need to look up the word 'immutable', perhaps 'adjudication' and acquire a nuanced understanding of the term 'engage' in this specific context – in other words, what it means 'to engage with' legal philosophy. Also, remember we talked about how legal philosophy, legal theory and jurisprudence are commonly used interchangeably. The term 'silent prologue' is a literary type of reference and so you need to find the original quote from Dworkin to ascertain the context within which it was used. You can do this by referring to the original source (*Law's Empire* is always available in the library as it is a seminal text), or you can find the quote in a secondary text (such as a journal, textbook or other scholarly text), or, if you are short of time, you could put the quote in a search engine.

Once you have done this you can begin to think about how to answer the question, and refer to the quotation as it resonates with other points you wish to make in your essay and/or as a way to introduce and/or conclude your essay. In other words, the degree to which the quotation is perceived to be important depends on (1) your interpretation and understanding of his words and context and (2) your agreement or otherwise with Dworkin's sentiments, and this will determine (3) how useful they are to you in answering the question as to whether jurisprudence is 'necessary' to discovering the nature of the law. A prologue is often an introductory or explanatory passage that establishes the setting for something else, so Dworkin is suggesting that legal philosophy is an unacknowledged necessary starting point, a necessary pre-interpretive stage (prior to determination of the content of rules or adjudication).

Important points to include

The assignment question is asking you to consider the importance of jurisprudence. Although there is always the option of arguing that jurisprudence is an irrelevance because the law is determinable on the basis of social fact and basic lawyering skills, we have learned that even this assertion belongs to a particular legal theory. In order to answer the question fully, you need to:

■ Explain why the question of 'what is law?' is not a simple matter of judicial precedent and statute.

■ Address the idea of law in context, as influenced by a range of considerations that may be interpreted as culturally, socially, theologically, politically or historically significant.

■ Explain how these belong to a set of distinctive schools of jurisprudential thought and how these categories help to order our understanding of the development, and hint at the future evolution, of law and legal concepts.

■ Finally, you could mention examples of issues from the past or modern issues that illustrate the continuing utility of jurisprudence, such as the grounds for permitting torture or possibilities for legalising assisted dying in the UK.

 Make your answer stand out

A distinctive answer will not only give a good, well-supported account, but will also make use of the vocabulary of jurisprudence. This means you should apply a few technical terms, such as 'hermeneutic', as well as attempting to use expressive language. A thesaurus is always helpful when writing this sort of essay, and will assist you in finding new ways of starting sentences and modes of expression. Think about using new terms that give a finer definition, more nuanced and closer to an exact expression of your idea. You can buy a hardcopy or ebook thesaurus version, or try one of the online free versions. There may be some expressions in this book that are unfamiliar, but once you have looked them up you will understand that they are really just different versions of a word you already understand. Students who are able to correctly interpret the assignment question in all aspects, and are able to articulate their findings, are those who are awarded the best grades.

READ TO IMPRESS

Bix, B.H. (2015) Overview, Purpose and Methodology, in *Jurisprudence: Theory and Context*, 7th edition. London: Sweet & Maxwell, 1–30.

Cotterrell, R. (2003) *The Politics of Jurisprudence: A Critical Introduction to Legal Philosophy*, 2nd edition. Oxford: Oxford University Press, 1–19.

Dworkin, R. (1998) *Law's Empire*. Oxford: Hart Publishing, 87–88, 225–275.

Freeman, M.D.A. (2014) Studying Jurisprudence in *Lloyd's Introduction to Jurisprudence*, 9th edition. London: Sweet & Maxwell, 1–74.

Goodrich, P. (1996) Of Blackstone's Tower: Metaphors of Distance and Histories of the English Law School, in *Pressing Problems in the Law Vol. II: What are Law Schools For?* P. Birks (ed.). Oxford: Oxford University Press, 59–68.

McBride, N. and Steel, S. (2014) The Value of Studying Jurisprudence, in *Great Debates in Jurisprudence*. London: Palgrave Macmillan, 232–248.

Sandel, M.J. (2010) Justice and the Common Good, in Justice: *What's the Right Thing to Do?* London: Penguin, 244–269.

Shaw, J.J.A. (2015) Compassion and the criminal justice system: stumbling along towards a jurisprudence of love and forgiveness. *International Journal of Law in Context*, 11(1): 92–107.

Twining, W. (2009) *General Jurisprudence: Understanding Law from a Global Perspective*. Cambridge: Cambridge University Press, 3–25.

www.pearsoned.co.uk/lawexpress

 Go online to access more revision support, including quizzes to test your knowledge, sample questions with answer guidelines, podcasts you can download and more!

Rights and justice

2

Revision checklist

Essential points you should know:

- [ ] The significance of the rhetoric of rights and justice to the development of legal theory
- [ ] The concept of natural rights and relevance of social contract theory
- [ ] Distinguishing between legal rights and moral rights
- [ ] Competing theories and analyses of rights
- [ ] What is justice? Four main theories
- [ ] Justice as fairness: the significance of Rawls' distributive theory of justice
- [ ] Nozick's theory of entitlements

■ Topic map

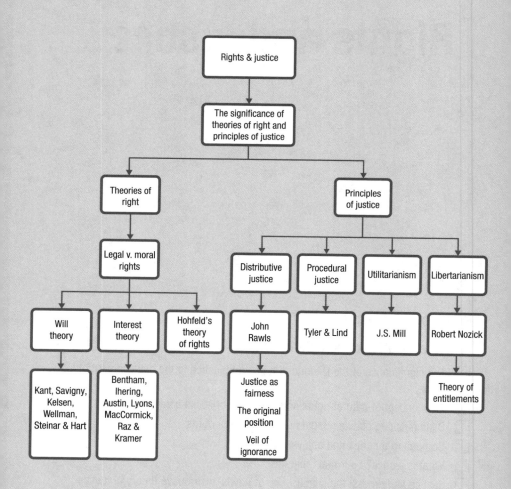

■ Introduction

What have theories of rights and justice got to do with the law?

A central characteristic of European thought has been the ideal of civilisation, based on respect for human dignity. This demands that each person has (as stated by Lord Lindsay, commenting on *Colonel Rainsborough's Observance 1647*) the fundamental and enduring right to plan and live his own life 'free from undue interference'. In an individualistic society, where people can exercise a high degree of subjective freedom in pursuit of their idea of a 'good life' based on their own values and life choices, it is necessary for law to demarcate the appropriate areas and provisions that can allow such liberty. For the same reason, it is also essential that law is able to provide limits – especially where unrestricted individual freedom would impinge on the freedom of others. In the absence of commonly shared values, this unbounded freedom would also apply to government officials and lead to, for example, the unacceptable use of discretion by public authorities; as in the case of *Malone* v *Metropolitan Police Commissioner* [1979] (see also *Malone* v *UK* [1979]). This is a convincing argument, which supports the provision of, at least, the minimum conditions for reciprocity and mutual respect within a pluralistic society, in order to guard against the emergence of an overly-general legal order in which everything that is not expressly forbidden is permitted.

A major area of concern within jurisprudence is how to determine the content, scope and appropriate protective mechanisms that are capable of upholding rights, in accordance with the ideal of justice. Questions arise, for example, relating to who (which individuals or groups) is capable of having rights and what subject matter can be deemed to be a right, and what level of protection is appropriate (or even possible) for upholding such rights. Some of these considerations are semantic, in that they turn on what the term 'right' signifies, beyond its dictionary definition. Consequently, it is necessary to establish not only 'what is a right' but also what can it mean 'to have a right to something', in relation to a competing right that in turn comprises part of a broader 'hierarchy of rights'. In other words, any discussion of rights within jurisprudence inevitably addresses the privileging of some rights over others, and seeks to determine the basis for these distinctions. The answers to such questions depend on the type of legal theory and theorist you choose to explain the phenomenon of rights within law.

Unlike the variant definitions of what constitutes a right, justice is considered to be a singular and universal concern. We tend to think of justice as overarching, standing above and beyond history, culture and tradition. Even where different societies have a variant idea of justice and legitimate all sorts of behaviour, these practices (such ►

as apartheid, which was until 1993 considered lawful under the terms of South Africa's constitutional provisions) often attract fierce criticism as they fail to meet with our commitment to a universal ideal and standard of justice. Both rights and justice are the subject of much debate within jurisprudence; also, the determination and protection of rights is commonly held to be inextricably bound together with the ideals of justice.

ASSESSMENT ADVICE

Essay questions on rights or justice will usually want you to show that you understand how these concepts both differ from and are an integral part of the development of foundational concepts as to the nature, function and purpose of the law. An essay question may ask you to evaluate competing rights claims or theories of justice on their merits – for example, by critical comparison of one theory against another. Alternatively, you may be asked to discuss the question of rights in the determination of options available for the terminally ill requesting medically assisted dying. This requires you to assess this ethical dilemma in the context of competing theories that allow maximum autonomy and choice against those that look at the good of society as a whole; also, in terms of the legitimacy of certain rights claims and how the assisted dying issue would be recast from a set of key theoretical positions.

Sample question

Could you answer this question? Below is a typical essay question that could arise on this topic. Guidelines on answering the question are included at the end of this chapter. Another sample question and guidance on tackling it can be found on the companion website.

ESSAY QUESTION

In *A Theory of Justice*, Rawls states that 'justice is the first virtue of social institutions'. Since justice is considered to be an important concept by most classical and contemporary theorists, why is it such a deeply contested area? Discuss.

■ Natural rights and social contract theory

In moral and political philosophy, the idea of acknowledging and safeguarding natural rights within a social contract originated in the Age of Enlightenment and was argued to be the consensual basis of legal and political authority. Natural rights are generally perceived as universal and *a priori*, or pre-existent; they are not created or defined by a sovereign authority but arise from a 'state of nature'. For Thomas Hobbes, the 'state of nature' meant all humans are born free and independent; they have a right to pursue their own self-interest and do not owe any duty to one another. Whereas for John Locke, the 'state of nature' meant that although society is not natural to humankind, it is the product of a social contract to which each individual must give their consent. Hobbes' social contract model privileges individual autonomy and absolute individual liberty (in other words 'take care of number one'), whilst Locke's model prioritises reciprocity and a duty to respect for the rights of others. There are a variety of conceptions. However, the social contract is essentially a mechanism for ensuring the recognition and protection of the natural rights of every citizen and, accordingly, legal duties and rights can exist only if they have been acknowledged and codified within the social contract.

Accordingly, social contract theory seeks to prove that law and justice arise only from agreement, and challenges the legitimacy of state authority over the individual. Significantly, the theory of social contract contradicts the aim of legal positivism in its quest to make law comprehensible without reference to the complex social, ethical and political aspects of the human condition. Legal positivists John Austin and Jeremy Bentham treated the notion of natural rights as irrational dogma and disregarded the social contract basis of sovereign authority, claiming, rather, that actual habitual obedience to state authority provided the factual basis of sovereign rule. Lawyers and the judiciary are, however, constantly faced with problems whose complexity cannot be fully understood by bare legal formula or the modification of juristic categories. Since law implies the existence of society, social contractarians claim that any philosophy of law must contain some basic assumptions about the nature of communal life, its organisation, institutions and purposes – and would inevitably address the tensions inherent in conflicting notions of liberty, equality, freedom, order and the legitimate use of power.

Key theories of natural rights and social contract advocated by, for example, Thomas Hobbes, John Locke and Jean-Jacques Rousseau went on to become the cornerstones of seventeenth- and eighteenth-century natural law theories. More recently, in *A Theory of Justice*, John Rawls uses a Kantian version of social contract theory to explain how political authority can only be justified by reference to an imagined and prior agreement between morally autonomous individuals. Each person is to have an equal right to the most extensive basic liberties, as compatible with liberties similar to those enjoyed by others; and socio-economic inequalities are to be addressed so that advantageous opportunities and positions are open to everyone. Assuming humans are capable of a common rationality, the principles of justice derived from that agreement or social contract would provide the ultimate criterion for the adjustment of the conflicting interests that are an integral part of social and legal experience.

Social contract theory

Social contract theory explains that the justification and purpose of the state is to establish a consensual system of sovereign authority, which recognises and upholds the natural rights of all individuals. In the absence of rules, and given unlimited freedom, it is purported that society would fragment and violent disorder would follow. For Hobbes, in a society where everyone looked out for themselves against every other person, life would become 'solitary, poor, nasty, brutish and short'. Society, therefore, functions according to a social contract, which is achieved by individuals grouping together for mutual protection and human flourishing, whilst voluntarily relinquishing some freedoms and agreeing to be subject to the law.

Legal rights v. moral rights

People act in particular ways, often on the sole basis that they are entitled to do so; whether or not their action is good or bad is immaterial. They may wish to consume only junk food, watch daytime television, stay out late every night after drinking 12 pints of beer and sleep in a hedge until sunrise on the basis of enforcing their 'right to party'. So, then, making a claim to perform a certain right does not have to be based on a good motive or the virtuous quality of that right; it is merely a taken-for-granted entitlement. In wider society there are competing rights claims, however, which strongly conflict with each other. People claim the right to life yet others claim the right to assisted dying and abortion; some may claim the right to information and a free press whilst others insist on prioritising the right to privacy. What we can recognise from the above examples is that rights claims are commonly claims to self-determination. Some of these rights claims are supported in law; for example, the right to life is enshrined in Article 2 of the European Convention on Human Rights and the Human Rights Act 1998. Alternatively, another example, the right to assisted dying is not legally sanctioned and is punishable under section 2 of the Suicide Act 1961, carrying a penalty of up to fourteen years in prison. The latter claim exemplifies the assertion of a moral right – facing certain death, the moral claim to the right to die with dignity in a manner and place of one's own choosing – which is unsupported by law and therefore not recognised as a legal right.

Western legal systems tend to support the idea of free choice whilst retaining their own right to exercise control, should someone choose to do something that conflicts with the imperative of maintaining social order and control. It is useful to define and try to distinguish between legal rights and moral rights. Legal rights claims are commonly based on recognised authoritative sources such as statute, judicial decisions or constitutional provisions, whereas moral rights are generally based on a moral theory that provides a set of moral norms. It may be argued that this is an arbitrary distinction because judges use their discretion in sentencing or awarding compensation, in which case the courts are not simply enforcing pre-existing legal rights: rather they are accommodating moral or social policy grounds. In this case the courts could be said to be, at least, recognising the validity of moral considerations and enforcing moral rights on the back of a pre-existing legal right. This is clearly common practice, since there are many examples of differing opinions that demonstrate that judges are inclined to particular interpretive techniques on the basis of their own personal ideological preferences.

Be critical

You need to remember that another charming characteristic of jurisprudence is the creation of categories with which to order certain legal propositions and the subsequent transgression of those carefully constructed boundaries. Your textbook may, for example, provide you with the distinguishing characteristics of moral and legal rights, only to then suggest that natural law theories often claim that legal rights are a peculiar kind of moral right. The key to enjoying jurisprudence is to remember that it is simply a form of inquiry into the nature of law – by asking a variety of probing questions, constructing classifications (theories of knowledge) from the answers and thereafter asking another question that either further develops or demolishes certain aspects of particular theories. Further questions arise sometimes as a response to new categories of culpability in relation to novel forms of crime or activity, such as cybercrime and identity theft or human cloning.

As a truly dynamic area of legal scholarship, it is hoped you can learn to love its quirky nature, because the critical character and refreshing dynamism of jurisprudence (always questioning and searching for new meaning, often in response to societal and cultural change) means you can be part of the evolutionary process by using relevant bits of theory to put together your own unique perspective on a particular issue or area of contention. At the level of asking a question such as 'can terrorism ever be justified?' or 'do terrorists have rights?', the answer depends on the depth of your own research by reference to different schools of jurisprudence, and how you frame key facets of your choice of appropriate theories with which to inform this important area of debate.

■ Main examples of rights theories and analyses

For Ronald Dworkin, in his 1977 *Taking Rights Seriously*, rights are best understood as the 'trumps' of an individual. This means if any individual right comes into conflict with any policy, the right must trump (or overcome), for example, any utilitarian or other collective justifications. He claims that rights offer reasons to treat their holders in a certain way or permit their holders to act in a certain manner, even if a laudable social aim would be served by doing otherwise. In other words, Dworkin believes that a right cannot be justifiably refused on policy grounds, even if refusing it would serve wider community interests.

'What is a right?' (in other words 'what should be the subject of a right?' and, by extension, 'what rights should people have?') is a thorny legal and moral question that creates considerable disagreement between legal theorists. You will notice that the separation of this question into two parts illustrates the difference between analytical and normative jurisprudential inquiry; however, you can also see how these two areas of inquiry are essentially connected. Rights are complex entities and there are two kinds of thought in this regard. Some legal theorists believe rights can be bounded by a precise terminology and fixed requirements that require no further explanation nor appeal to any higher moral measure. Other theorists assume certain conclusions flow from the demands that are made through the exercise of the right, which means they have 'peremptory force'. There are juridical consequences from such rights claims, as each has an internal complexity and forms part of a system of realms of liberty, towards realising a shared ideal of freedom. Immanuel Kant exemplifies this perspective.

Drawing on his *Metaphysics of Morals*, Kant insists that the rules and principles of justice are founded on reason, and all citizens possess equal rights, not least of all because a distinctive characteristic of human agency is the capacity for freedom and the exercise of free will. This means that the possession of a right entitles the holder to act in a particular way and that people have a duty not to interfere with that right; the corollary of which is that coercion is justified in order to protect that right. This perspective falls within the category of *will theory* (choice theory). Other famous will theorists include Savigny, Kelsen, Wellman, Steiner and Hart, who stated that right-holders wield power over another's duty, making them 'small scale sovereigns'. *Interest theory* (benefit theory) is in disagreement with this definition of rights; rather, it maintains that the function of a right is to advance the right-holder's interests.

Interest theory

Interest theorists believe that an owner has a right, not because owners have choices, but because ownership of that right makes the owner better off and is, therefore, in their best interests. This means that positive law-making is responsible for ordering those interests, as they cannot be reconciled and rendered mutually consistent. Interest theorists include, for example, Bentham, Ihering, Austin, Lyons, MacCormick, Raz and Kramer.

 Make your answer stand out

You need to remember that jurisprudence is an argumentative discipline and the rights question is a common source of contention. There is no ideal perspective and no consensus on which theory of the functions and purpose of rights is the correct one, or indeed whether we ought to believe that rights have any function in law at all. It is, however, important that when writing essays or answering examination questions, you demonstrate your familiarity with the key theorists in this area, and their main points of difference.

Will theory

Will theory is primarily associated with H.L.A. Hart and gives the right-holder exclusive control over another individual's duty, in relation to the performance of that right. There are no exceptions, no unwaivable rights. This means that since rights always confer sovereignty, these cannot be acknowledged in the case of 'incompetents', or those who are incapable of exercising sovereignty. For example, infants, animals and comatose adults cannot have rights under this theory. Critics, such as MacCormick, have argued against the value of will (or 'choice') theory on the grounds that the right not to be enslaved or tortured has to extend to everyone, including the excluded categories mentioned above.

Many definitions and categories of rights are proposed by legal theorists. American jurist, Wesley Hohfeld, found that respected theorists will even use variant meanings of the word 'right' in the same sentence. He wrote that such imprecision of language indicated a concomitant imprecision of thought, which adversely impinged on the resulting legal conclusions. To tackle this confusion borne of imprecise definitions and understandings, he determined to clarify any talk of rights by breaking the term 'rights' down into four distinct concepts. Hohfeld's analysis of rights is one of the most important theories and is often used as a starting point for considering the question of rights in jurisprudence.

Hohfeld's theory of rights

Hohfeld offers a typology of opposites and correlatives, which he refers to as the 'lowest common denominators of the law', and presents as essential in order to avoid judicial confusion. The four 'jural relations' are (1) rights, as claims, (2) liberties, or privileges, (3) powers and (4) immunities. These all represent forms of rights that are opposite to each other: for example, a right is a claim against another person whereas a liberty or privilege frees one from such a claim. Furthermore, one has legal power over another person whereas immunity represents one's freedom from that legal power.

In addition, Hohfeld provides the legal position entailed for the other party due to the exercise of the above four types of right. In other words, if a person has a right to something, another person may have an incumbent duty to perform an action or a duty to desist from doing something to negate the force of that right. If an individual is at liberty to do something, such as wear a tinfoil hat, then another person has no right to stop them from doing so, neither does that person have also to wear a tinfoil hat.

It should be noted that these fundamental Hohfeldian rights are best understood simply as rights against another individual, so they resolve only one issue that arises between two parties. This is a definitional or stipulative theory and not based on empirical evidence; however, it offers a clear understanding of what rights we have in a range of different circumstances, and suggests what the consequences of holding a particular Hohfeldian entitlement or burden would be.

What is justice?

Jurisprudence is concerned with the nature of law and justice. As is the case with other notions arising within legal theory, some theorists claim that the concept of justice has no inherent substantive content. Critics argue that discussions about justice have little merit as they only present areas of conflict between justice theorists who, in turn, merely champion their own preferred content. Alternatively, there are others who believe the question of justice is, and ought to be, a major area of concern and theoretical investigation. This follows the classical philosophical tradition led by Plato, Aristotle, Kant and Hegel. More recently, John Finnis declared that the object of the principles of justice is to achieve the common good for all in a particular society. In *Natural Law and Natural Rights* he states that the complex theories and 'language of rights' are no more than 'a supple and potentially precise instrument for sorting out and expressing the demands of justice'. This is, of course, a complex task as there are many definitions of what is a common good, and what are the conditions that would enable practical reasonableness to bring about 'human flourishing'. The distribution of natural resources and the allocation of rights in (and allowing access to) communally owned goods, for instance, are important considerations. Justice is undeniably an important legal concept and aim, and it is the object of jurisprudence to attempt to classify and categorise those conflicting concepts of what justice means (according to either a narrower or wider set of objects, conditions and priorities) and not least of all to provide a coherent basis for the legitimate use of legal authority.

KEY DEFINITION: Four main theories of justice

- **Distributive justice** relates to the development of normative principles that can lead to the fair or socially just distribution of goods – for example, power, wealth, reward, privileges and respect – according to the merits of the individual and the best interests of society. Any discussion of this theory of justice usually begins with the work of John Rawls in his seminal work, *A Theory of Justice*.

- **Procedural justice** is concerned with the idea of the principle of fairness in relation to the mechanisms and processes that facilitate the allocation of goods and resources, as well as the fairness of dispute resolution processes – as opposed to the mere fact of equal distribution. The idea is that if a transparent and fair process is used to decide on the distribution of goods, then people may even accept an imbalance in what they receive by comparison to others. Modern theorists such as Tyler and Lind and Thibaut and Walker have proposed a variety of models of procedural justice.

- **Utilitarianism** is identified with the writing of Jeremy Bentham and J.S. Mill, and determines that the moral worth of an action, rule or principle can only be judged by its outcome. The individual as a distinct entity is ignored in favour of prioritising the promotion of collective human welfare, namely 'the greatest good for the greatest number'. The distribution of goods and resources is not the priority; what matters is how much good for the majority can be produced. A theory of justice is derived from what is considered 'good' or right, as happiness or welfare, by mainstream society. Utilitarians refer to the maximisation of good as the 'principle of utility' and disagree on what can be considered good or right. History is irrelevant as this theory is purely forward-looking, in that utilitarianism seeks to determine what actions will have the best consequences for all concerned.

- **Libertarianism** or 'entitlement theory' understands justice to be a purely historical issue in that, as Robert Nozick has stated, 'whether a distribution is just depends on how it came about'. Most libertarians would reject the idea that there ought to be any principles that govern the distribution of resources, since the distribution of income and wealth is dependent upon the free choices of autonomous individuals, who have equal access to basic liberties. So, then, libertarians consider the free market to be inherently just, and that redistributive taxation would be a violation of people's property rights.

■ *Justice as fairness*: the enduring significance of the Rawls theory of distributive justice

There are elements of Kant's moral philosophy in Rawls' theory of distributive justice, not least of all his method of morally evaluating political and social institutions. In 1971 Rawls published *A Theory of Justice*, which aims to consider the concept in terms of what we already know and believe about justice, and what we would consider to be a 'right action' or morally right view after weighing up all the alternatives from, for example, general judgements and specific principles. The outcome of this process of inductive reasoning is referred to by Rawls as *reflective equilibrium* – in other words, the end point of a deliberative process in which we have reflected upon and revised our intuitions and beliefs about an area of moral or non-moral inquiry. Rawls considers this to be the best starting point for thinking about questions of justice because human beings have an innate 'sense of justice' that is both a source of moral judgement and moral motivation.

The method of reflective equilibrium serves the purpose of outlining a realistic and stable social order by shaping a practically coherent set of principles that are grounded in the right way – namely, in the source of our moral motivation, such that all people (as rational moral agents) could regard them as authoritative and comply with them. Rawls offers a model of a fair choice situation, introducing his conceptual framework of the **original position** along with its necessary **veil of ignorance**, within which parties would hypothetically choose mutually agreeable principles of justice.

KEY DEFINITION: The original position

Rawls envisages a hypothetical original position from which rational human beings are able to decide which conditions are favourable to impose on people and organise a just society. This is achieved by social cooperation, in which people imagine themselves as free and equal, and then jointly agree upon and commit themselves to determining the principles of social and political justice. Unlike Rousseau's idea of a social contract, however, people in the original position come together without knowing where or how they will eventually stand in the society they have agreed to accept. Their position in society is not settled until the structure of society has been agreed.

KEY DEFINITION: The veil of ignorance

The veil of ignorance ensures impartiality as people are unaware of status, class, race, natural ability, privilege or wealth; therefore, 'justice as fairness' is assured along with a unanimous result because everyone's interests are uniformly reconciled. They are aware of the existence of society, history, economics, biology, for example, and the possible characteristics of society's members, as intelligent, gendered and so on; however, they would not be able to determine individual cases on those grounds. Behind the veil of ignorance, any knowledge of individual distinguishing features is excluded. All decisions made in this way would be authoritative and binding.

Rawls argues that by a process of reflective equilibrium or deliberation, according to the 'original position' and the 'veil of ignorance', people would strongly favour his two preferred principles of justice over other possible contenders. This is because both offer conceptions of justice that best advance the interests of the parties in establishing conditions that enable them to effectively pursue their final ends and fundamental interests.

His first principle of justice, the *Principle of Equal Liberty*, states that each person is to be granted the greatest degree of basic liberties that is consistent with granting similar liberties for everyone. Following on, his second principle, the *Difference Principle*, states that practices that produce social and economic inequalities among individuals are allowable (a) only if they work out to everyone's advantage, including those least advantaged, and (b) if the positions and offices that come with greater reward are equally open to everyone. Rawls' two stable principles of justice are only possible because of the collectively natural and unbiased 'original position' starting point of deliberation and because, like Kant, he believes our nature is expressed according to moral principles.

The justice of any system depends upon how rights and duties are distributed, and on the equality of opportunity and social conditions in a particular society. Rawls is attempting to construct a methodology from which to derive principles of justice, capable of bringing about a consensus on how society can be organised fairly according to the best possible arrangement of primary social and political goods. Rawls' concept of justice as fairness could, therefore, be summed up as egalitarian liberalism, based upon a hypothetical social contract.

 Make your answer stand out

Show you are familiar with the terminology of rights and justice theorists – for example, by explicitly referring to Rawls' 'veil of ignorance' and 'original position'. These are complex terms that underpin his philosophy of justice as fairness, and you need to be able to understand and demonstrate the full implications of these definitions, relate them to his overall thesis and to our understanding of justice as modern lawyers in a more general sense.

■ Nozick's free market libertarianism

Although both Nozick and Rawls regard utilitarianism as an inadequate means of measuring justice, a large proportion of Robert Nozick's 1974 *Anarchy, State, and Utopia* is dedicated to refuting Rawls' theory of justice as deeply flawed by, for example, asserting that his principles of liberty and difference contradict each other. Nozick claims his theory is morally grounded because it advocates respect for free will and the right to self-determination. This particular theory of justice is based on property ownership, and Nozick maintains that a just state cannot realise any pattern of distribution without violating individual rights. Any government that forcibly taxes the rich and redistributes their wealth to assist the poor, therefore, violates the liberty of the rich and negates their hard work or talent in accumulating these rewards. He also suggests that individuals will inevitably undermine any proposed pattern of distribution by engaging in transactions and transfers that can be deemed just, but defy the Rawlsian theory of justice and render it unworkable.

Nozick upholds the rights of the individual, and advocates a minimal state or 'night-watchman' state to maintain law and order; which would entail a government that offers protection (by the use of legislation, the courts and enforcement agencies) against coercive force, fraud and theft, but would not would attempt to control or regulate an individual's actions beyond this point. His work defends the principles of free market libertarianism and his Entitlement Theory is grounded on the notion that only free market exchanges respect people as equals, as 'ends in themselves'. The rights and principles endorsed by Nozick are historical, in that the justice of a particular holding depends upon the history of how that holding came to be held. So, if a person's current holdings are justly acquired, then the transfer principle alone determines whether subsequent distributions are just. His critics claim that it is unclear why the initial holders were able to exclude others from this position of privilege – that is, how were some able to become landowners and others only land workers? In other words, Nozick does not consider the effect of alternative methods of distribution and simply instantiates the morally dubious criterion of 'who is first, wins'.

KEY THEORY

Nozick's theory of entitlements

Nozick justifies the free market, even if it does not produce optimal justice, on the basis of three distinct principles:

1. The *Transfer Principle* asserts that holdings (including voluntary exchange and gifts) that are freely acquired from others who also acquired them in a just way are justly acquired.

2. The *Acquisition Principle* asserts that people are entitled to holdings that have been initially acquired in a just way.

3. The *Rectification Principle* outlines how to rectify violations of principles 1 and 2 above; where, for example, holdings may have been unjustly transferred or acquired by individuals or the government. Remedies may include compensation and restoration of property in order to rectify past injustices.

Be critical

Think about how these theories of right and justice have been formulated (on what basis, according to what criteria, for example) and discuss their applicability (or otherwise) to modern society. For example, you might mention how Nozick's theory of entitlements can be perceived in light of the recent financial sector crisis and lack of regulation. Then you can compare a Rawlsian perspective and consider how this alternative view may inform the same scenario.

! Don't be tempted to . . .

Although analysis of the theories of justice and rights would hopefully inform the development of theories of criminal justice and human rights legislation, they are separate topics with a different area of inquiry. Theories of criminal justice are concerned with punishment of the wrongdoer and are traditionally one of the main themes of criminology, which is the theoretical branch of criminal law. Human rights is often connected with the law of civil liberties, which considers the doctrine of human rights in international practice, international law, global and regional institutions, as well as in the policies of states and activities of non-governmental organisations. The language of rights and justice is often relevant in each case but the focus is different.

Also, be sure to keep your analysis objective and don't be tempted to drift into giving your preferred view on the validity or coherence of the different theories. Remember you are comparing the theories (on the basis of relevant premises) to each other and this is the basis for your critique – not personal opinion. Of course you may lean towards one theory against another, but this will be apparent by means of your carefully constructed analysis of the key propositions against the alternatives.

■ Putting it all together

Answer guidelines

See the sample question at the start of the chapter.

Approaching the question

Acknowledging the quote from Rawls, and since law is inarguably a social institution, you are being asked to explain why theories of justice are essential to understanding the nature, function and purpose of law. You will want to begin by considering the purported aims of theories and principles of justice and outline the scope of inquiry according to the main contribution and characteristics of each key theory in this area. Consideration of some bold statements made by key legal theorists, for example, John Finnis, will be useful. He claimed that 'fostering the common good of the community as a general requirement' is the aim of justice. You can critically compare this type of statement with those made by other theorists, who may prioritise alternative goals and assignment of goods and services in order to ensure social cohesion. The identification and recognition of legitimate objects and rights holders, as well as levels of protection attaching to particular rights claims, are some of the key aims of justice; in other words, the type of rights that can be claimed, by whom and subject to what conditions, are all areas for explication within your essay.

Important points to include

- The credibility of Rawls' thesis has often been called into question, possibly because he has provided the most comprehensive argument to date for a theory of justice – so, even in a generic essay question on justice, this should be a key starting point and basis for comparison.

- Consider competing theses from key thinkers and key theories, as indicated in earlier sections of this chapter.

- If the essay question is issue-driven, or you want to incorporate a more fundamental starting point for your deliberation such as explicating 'the language of rights', then you might refer to some of the non-traditional theories arising from within the Critical Legal Theory tradition (see Chapter 8).

- The Critical Legal body (such as Feminist and Critical Race theorists) have criticised mainstream theories of right and justice on the basis that these are too often incoherent and indeterminate, limit the human imagination within narrowly conceived 'discourses of rights' and may even impede progress towards genuine democracy and justice.

- The addition of this line of inquiry would also provide a critical point of departure from simply addressing the significance of solely traditional theories of right and justice.

Make your answer stand out

This is a theme that is characterised by memorable quotations and unfamiliar terminology, which arises within a wide variety of disciplinary contexts, from economic to philosophical. Legal theorists have devised their own distinct forms of expression with which to explain the nuances of their theoretical positions. Rather than merely describing these, the only way to get a first-class mark is to understand where these definitions come from (historically and culturally), what aspects of social life they relate to (categories of rights), who can hold these rights and how they are distributed, and policed. These are all pertinent considerations and you will need to use a good range of supporting material in your answer.

READ TO IMPRESS

Campbell, T. (2006) *Rights: A Critical Introduction*. Abingdon, Oxford: Routledge, 43–61.

Coyle, S. (2014) *Justice, Law and History in Modern Jurisprudence: A Philosophical Guide*, 1–18, 241–245.

Douzinas, C. and Gearey, A. (2005) *Critical Jurisprudence: The Political Philosophy of Justice*. Oxford: Hart Publishing, 107–139.

Dworkin, R.M. (1977) *Justice and Rights, in Taking Rights Seriously*. Cambridge, Mass: Harvard University Press, 185–222.

Dworkin, R.M. (2013) *Justice for Hedgehogs*. Cambridge, MA: Harvard University Press, 1–22.

Penner, J. and Melissaris, E. (2012) *McCoubrey & White's Textbook on Jurisprudence*, 5th edition. Oxford: Oxford University Press, 183–197.

Riley, S. (2013) *Legal Philosophy*. Harlow: Pearson Education, 130–137, 151–159.

Simmonds, N.E. (2013) *Central Issues in Jurisprudence: Justice, Law and Rights*, 4th edition. London: Sweet & Maxwell, 277–302.

Veitch, S., Christodoulidis, E. and Farmer, L. (2012) *Jurisprudence: Themes and Concepts*, 2nd edition. Abingdon: Routledge, 50–64.

www.pearsoned.co.uk/lawexpress

 Go online to access more revision support, including quizzes to test your knowledge, sample questions with answer guidelines, podcasts you can download and more!

Law and morality

3

Revision checklist

Essential points you should know:

- [ ] What is morality?
- [ ] The importance of morality to legal theorists
- [ ] The significance of the complex relationship between law and morality
- [ ] *The Case of the Speluncean Explorers*: can we justify eating people?
- [ ] Conflicting perspectives 1: the *Hart* v *Fuller* debate – natural law v. positivist view
- [ ] Conflicting perspectives 2: *Hart* v *Devlin* – the enforcement of morality
- [ ] Conflicting perspectives 3: *Hart* v *Devlin* – private v. public morality

■ Topic map

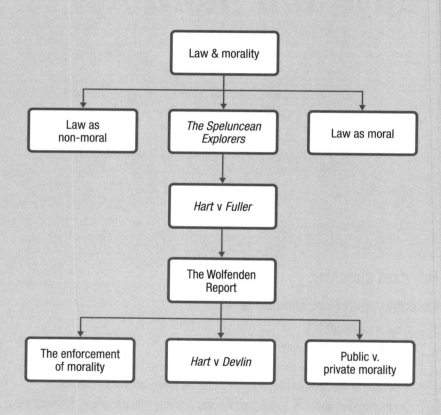

▮ Introduction

Law and morality: the good, the bad and the ugly

This is an area of continuing disagreement; the debate relating to the connection between law and morality brings out the good, the bad and the downright ugly in warring legal theorists. Normative disciplines such as law seek to define their territory according to simple categories that establish absolute principles purporting to offer a single truth as to what is just and unjust, right and wrong, good and bad. A study of jurisprudence demonstrates how the determination of these categories is anything but simple. Invariably questions of right and justice will necessitate the discussion of values (that is, what is good or bad is often a moral evaluation) and for many people this means morality is a central concern.

The relationship between law and morality continues to be one of the main areas of conflict between natural lawyers and legal positivists because each opposing view is equally plausible. On one hand, it is possible to view questions relating to the existence of law and rules as different from, and not dependent upon, the moral acceptability of law. On the other hand, there are many examples that demonstrate the extent to which law is intrinsically loaded with moral content. This is evident in the legal concepts of responsibility, fault, compensation and duty; indeed, Dworkin claims that every action at law has an inescapable moral dimension. Lord Steyn also stated in *McFarlane and Another* v *Tayside Health Board* [1999] 4 All ER 977 that although courts of law are not courts of morals, the judiciary's 'sense of the moral answer to a question, or the justice of a case, has been one of the great shaping forces of the common law'.

ASSESSMENT ADVICE

An essay or examination question will require you to make reference to key competing legal theories/theorists, and how they define and delimit the role of morality in law. Although some theorists claim that law is morally neutral and that there is no *essential* connection between law and morality, even legal positivists have been forced to concede that particularly difficult ethical dilemmas can only be explained by resorting to moral evaluations in judgment. Others provide counter arguments indicating a consistent complex interaction between law and morality, and that many laws and legal practices rely on a nuanced set of moral reasons and justifications. You may need to illustrate the role of morality in legal theory by providing examples from legal practice, perhaps by addressing the implications of a complicated moral dilemma such as 'can killing ever be justified?'. There are many examples you can choose from to illustrate the necessary overlap between law and moral considerations – for example, those pivotal moral issues arising in *Airedale National Health Services Trust* v *Bland* [1993] 2WLR 316 within the context of euthanasia.

■ Sample question

Could you answer this question? Below is a typical essay question that could arise on this topic. Guidelines on answering the question are included at the end of this chapter. Another sample question and guidance on tackling it can be found on the companion website.

ESSAY QUESTION

In his seminal work *The Enforcement of Morals*, Devlin posed the question: 'What is the connection between crime and sin and to what extent, if at all, should the criminal law of England concern itself with the enforcement of morals and punish sin or immorality as such?' Discuss.

■ Why is morality important?

Bearing in mind that law is committed to providing a minimum standard of justice, for certain legal theorists this means that, by its very nature, law is obliged to have clear moral aims. In the absence of a moral core, they believe law must be unjust or, as for John Finnis, fail to serve the common good or, as for Ronald Dworkin, fail to justify rightful coercion. These laws may be considered as value-free and therefore unworthy of our obedience; however, there are laws that have no moral content and merely aim to consolidate power or turn a profit, yet these are still legitimate. For example, Parliament may enact anti-social or environmentally unfriendly laws or choose to ignore moral considerations by failing to regulate the behaviour of its officials, as is the recent case with the finance and banking industries. Whether through bad faith a law has no moral content, or a policy of deliberate non-regulation brings hardship upon mainstream society, the legal community acts in a way that assumes the moral high ground. Even in these circumstances, moral virtue is perceived as an important characteristic and one that all legal actors seek to claim for themselves.

Law has been described as having the moral authority to coerce; also, moral considerations become pertinent especially when we can recognise a genuine legal obligation, yet determine there are other moral factors that have greater authority. Inarguably, morality is important to legal theory and legal practice. So how can we define morality? First of all, the term 'ethics' is sometimes used interchangeably with morality; however, ethics relates to the narrower field of codes of conduct and chosen moral principles of specific groups or organisations. There are many variants of morality in a general sense, for example: *personal morality*, which is based on subjective feeling and experience; *conventional morality*, which often adheres to a set of social mores and conventions; and *critical morality*, which outlines a set of moral standards by which to judge political and social conventions. Immanuel Kant's **deontological** formulation of the 'categorical imperative' is based on the notion of duty, in that an actor must freely choose impartially conceived moral maxims (or reasons given for legitimating a certain action), which, because of their moral content, can ideally be applied to everyone in the same circumstances without contradiction or exception. According to John Finnis, moral action is justified not because of having knowledge of human nature, but rather from knowing what are 'worthwhile ends' or aims. The assumption that particular moral virtues exist independently of our minds or convention, and that we ought to act on these, constitutes what is referred to as **moral realism**.

KEY DEFINITION: Deontological

Deontological moral theories come in a variety of forms, but the main thrust is the concept of duty and the rightness of action (making the correct moral choices) in relation to a moral rule as to whether the action is morally required, forbidden or permitted. Kant's theory of moral philosophy is considered deontological because, first, people must act in a morally virtuous way from duty (rather than desire) and, secondly, only the motives of the actor make the action moral, not the outcome of the action.

■ Can we justify eating people?

Lon Fuller's fictional legal case, *The Case of the Speluncean Explorers*, is over fifty years old yet it remains one of the classic allegorical examples of the diversity of jurisprudential attitudes, which are still exhibited by the judiciary in modern times. The exploration of important moral issues raised by the case highlights the purposes for which the law exists, and this is the sort of complex issue that continues to trouble legal and moral philosophers. The facts: trapped in a cave, the men decide to draw lots and cannibalise one of their number to survive until rescuers can reach them. The State's murder statute states 'whoever shall wilfully take the life of another shall be punished by death' and the judges must decide whether to apply the mandatory sentence (hanging) or find grounds to create an exception to an otherwise categorical rule. It is based on the real lifeboat cases of *U.S.* v *Holmes* [1842] and *Regina* v *Dudley and Stephens* [1884], in which tragedy at sea was followed by a killing and prosecution; in *Holmes*, the killing was to lighten an overloaded lifeboat and in *Dudley and Stephens*, the reason was to provide a meal for the ravenous survivors. The conflicting legal judgments each represent very different approaches to legal reasoning.

The Chief Justice's opinion tends towards seeking a pardon against conviction and sentence, whilst Judge Tatting evades responsibility by abstaining from making a decision. Judge Keen exhibits the characteristics of legal positivism by insisting on a strict separation of the issues of law and morality; his deliberation presents a view of law as warped, overly authoritarian and oppressive. Judge Handy prioritises conventional morality, administrative convenience and cohesion. Judge Foster (representing Fuller) looks to the significance of the 'spirit' rather than the 'letter of the law' and champions a belief in the necessity for law, morality and reason to coalesce in deciding, in this instance, difficult legal questions. Finally, Fuller seeks to combine these differing views into eight principles comprising 'the inner morality of law'; these would assure the promulgation of only just laws, with general applicability, which would recognise and meet the demands of morality.

Fuller's morality of law

In his 1964 *The Morality of Law*, Fuller distinguished between two obligatory moralities. The first he called 'aspiration', which relates to maximal human achievement and the goal of excellence; this corresponds to the desires and needs of individuals that would also serve the collective best interest. The second morality, 'duty', suggests a minimum standard of rule adherence (without stipulating any content), just enough from the individual to ensure the orderly functioning of society. Citizens can aspire to achieving higher status or certain aims, but first they must agree to accept the terms of the minimum baseline from which to fulfil their aspirations. The main focus is on process – in other words, how law is made as opposed to its actual content – on the basis that laws that are consistent would be fair and therefore more effective than laws that do not meet the eight criteria of **Fuller's 'inner morality of law'**.

KEY DEFINITION: Fuller's *inner morality of law*

Fuller offers eight key measures to ensure that law-making adheres to a minimum standard. If a law exhibits all aspects, it is then considered to be good (or moral) law:

- Promulgation of the law, so its rules and principles can be known in advance
- It must be possible to perform, and not make demands that are beyond the capacities of its citizens
- No retroactive legislation
- No contradictions or ambiguities in the law
- It must be clear, accessible and easy to understand
- No ad hoc or inconsistent adjudication, due to a lack of adequate rules
- No frequent introduction of amendments, so rules are stable
- There must be congruence between the rules as announced and their actual administration.

■ *Hart* v *Fuller* debate: a natural law v. positivist perspective

The relationship between law and morality has erupted over various key societal events, such as the laws of Nazi Germany in the Second World War and the apartheid policies of the South African government, which only ceased in 1994. The debate between modern legal positivist H.L.A. Hart and procedural natural lawyer L.L. Fuller illustrates some of the tensions between those promoting the necessary moral quality of law over those who privilege legal validity; culminating in Hart's publication of his 1961 *The Concept of Law* and Fuller's (1969 revised edition) *The Morality of Law*.

Hart expressed his conviction that a legal system did not need to be moral or satisfy some requirement for justice in order to be legitimate. He used the example of Nazism to illustrate that since their policies on racial distinctions were relevant, applied consistently and that discrimination reflected the views of that society, this was still a legal system. It was fully functional in spite of being neither just nor moral: on this basis Hart claimed it was necessary to separate the question of what constitutes law from what is moral or just (which accords with the positivistic 'separation thesis'). Alternatively, Fuller believed Nazi laws did not meet the criteria of law (found in his eight principles), nor indeed were they lawful, being instruments of arbitrariness and repression. The *Hart* v *Fuller* debate centred on a so-called 'grudge case', which arose after the end of the Second World War and related to people who had used oppressive Nazi legislation (which was valid at the time) to settle scores or personal grudges by becoming a 'grudge informer', with the result that their victim would be severely punished or even killed.

KEY EXAMPLE

The case of the 'grudge informer'

During the Second World War, a German woman who wished to get rid of her soldier husband had denounced him to the authorities on the grounds of making derogatory remarks about Hitler (despite having no legal duty to do so) in accordance with the anti-sedition regulations of 1934 and 1938. The husband was prosecuted and convicted of criticising the Reich and potentially harming its defence, which carried the death penalty. Although sentenced to death, he was reprieved and posted to the Eastern front. He survived the war and on returning home, in 1949, instituted proceedings against his wife and the judge, claiming he had been unlawfully deprived of his liberty under the 1871 German Criminal Code, paragraph 239. The judge was found not guilty, having made the decision under a then-valid yet inhuman law. The woman protested her innocence, claiming she had acted in accordance with the law (the informer statutes); however, she was found guilty because her actions were borne of personal malice. Also, the Appeal Court found the statutes were 'contrary to the sound conscience and sense of justice of all decent human beings'.

Hart and Fuller both conceded that evil legal systems are unlikely to flourish, not least of all because the allegiance of the people depends upon the coercive powers of an oppressive regime. Although Hart also agreed that the actions of grudge informers were worthy of punishment, he maintained that retrospective legislation should have been used for this purpose rather than relying upon the invalidating effect of immorality. Fuller disagreed, criticising the positivist stance to separate legal obligation from all other types of obligation, for example, moral duty. Post-Second World War, Fuller insisted the judges must entertain reasonable moral questions in order to construct a legitimate legal order.

 Make your answer stand out

Many authors, such as Dworkin and Cotterrell, have offered different views on this famously heated *Hart* v *Fuller* debate in their own work. You might use such comments in support of your own assertions. In his book, *The Politics of Jurisprudence*, Roger Cotterrell states, 'there is often a sense that in the battle of arguments no one ever wins, and further that there are no reliable criteria by which one could recognize victory anyway. The disputes seem timeless, the issues never resolved.' This quotation can also summarise the intractability or inherent difficulty of resolving abstract issues, such as those raised within jurisprudential inquiry.

■ *Hart* v *Devlin* I: the enforcement of morality

The prolonged debate between H.L.A. Hart and prominent British judge and jurist Lord Patrick Devlin came about after the publication of the 1957 *Report of the Departmental Committee on Homosexual Offences and Prostitution* (Cmnd 247), more famously known as the Wolfenden Report. The Report recommended the decriminalisation of homosexuality between consenting adults; female homosexuality (lesbianism) was not viewed as a criminal activity. It further stated that 'unless a deliberate attempt is to be made by society, acting through the agency of the law, to equate the sphere of crime with that of sin, there must remain a realm of private morality and immorality which is, in brief and crude terms, not the law's business'.

After all, there are many 'sins' such as fornication, adultery and telling lies that may conflict with one's sense of morality, but at the same time these are not crimes and do not attract criminal sanction. The Wolfenden Committee sought to apply the same logic and extend it to include homosexuality, which was, until the 1967 Sexual Offences Act, a criminal offence under the 1861 Offences Against the Person Act law on sodomy and the accompanying 1885

Labouchere Amendment. Devlin vehemently disagreed and wanted a continuation of the anti-sodomy laws, whilst Hart espoused the view that it was not the proper role of criminal law to dissolve the idea of selfhood and the capacity for free choice, by the enforcement of a particular set of morals and morality.

 Make your answer stand out

It is important to understand the importance of the Wolfenden Committee's recommendation that 'homosexual behaviour between consenting adults in private should no longer be a criminal offence'. This is a significant development in the area of law and morality, and you should be familiar with the findings of the report and how these apply to the public v. private debate. You should also be able to discuss how the report applies utilitarian philosopher J.S. Mill's 'harm principle' by claiming that in matters of private morality, the individual has the capacity to make free choices in which the law has no right to interfere: 'The law's function is to preserve public order and decency, to protect the citizen from what is offensive or injurious, and to provide sufficient safeguards against exploitation and corruption of others … It is not, in our view, the function of the law to intervene in the private life of citizens, or to seek to enforce any particular pattern of behaviour.'

In his 1958 Maccabean lecture to the British Academy entitled 'The Enforcement of Morals', which articulated **Devlin's concept of moral legalism**, Lord Devlin publicly opposed the recommendations of the Wolfenden Report. He argued that, if they were to be adopted, it would eliminate a number of specific crimes, such as passive and, more controversially, active euthanasia, suicide pacts and incest, as these are all acts that can be done in private by consenting adults without giving offence or corrupting the morals of others. Devlin warned of the disintegrating effect of a lapse in enforcing moral standards and appealed to the idea of society resting upon a shared morality as a 'seamless web' that must be able to defend itself against a subversive act against its moral structure. He feared that any attack on society's constitutive morality would lead to the inevitable disintegration of society; 'the suppression of vice is as much the law's business as the suppression of subversive activities'. As a corollary of this view, he claimed there should be no limit to the reach of law's influence in moral matters, and he championed a 'jury box' morality based on the morals of the ordinary 'right-minded' person who has the ability to discern what constitutes an immoral act.

KEY DEFINITION: Devlin's concept of moral legalism

Devlin rejected the distinction between public and private morality, claiming that the protection of morals in the public interest is more powerful than the protection of the individual freedom of consenting parties in an immoral act. To this end, he proposed three guiding principles that would enable the interests of private individuals to be balanced against the public requirements of society:

- Law should support a maximum standard of individual freedom as far as compatible with social integrity.

- Law should only intervene when society, the 'right-minded' citizenry, refuses to tolerate certain behaviour. As society progresses, tolerance may vary so law should be slow to change its moral stance.

- Privacy should be respected, but those interests must be balanced with the need for law to be enforced in the face of internal or external threats.

Be critical

The judiciary believes it is justified in constructing itself as a moral arbiter (as per Lord Devlin), drawing a line between what is acceptable and unacceptable in civil society. Critically evaluate the grounds on which law has silenced certain minority groups, or pathologised particular issues (such as equating homosexuality with disease, or pregnancy out of wedlock being indicative of mental illness), and to what extent this has either protected society or impeded debate. In the UK, abortion and suicide were (prior to the 1960s) considered to be wicked acts and did not merit wider discussion by the legal community. Compare the grounds on which competing legal theories set up the important law v. morality, private v. public debate.

■ *Hart* v *Devlin* II: public v. private morality

Hart was sceptical about Devlin's social cohesion/shared morality arguments (which fail to define what is meant by 'society') and doubted that populist views could be relied upon to be always correct or morally grounded: 'The central mistake is a failure to distinguish the acceptable principle that political power is best entrusted to the majority from the unacceptable claim that what the majority do with that power is beyond criticism and must never be resisted.' He invoked J.S. Mill's 'harm principle' in his argument, which stipulates, in the absence of harm to society, that the government has no right to intrude on the lives of individuals (with the exception of vulnerable individuals such as those lacking capacity, the young and infirm); adding that not all moral developments indicate a disintegration of society.

More significantly, in his 1963 *Law, Liberty and Morality*, Hart criticised the tradition of 'judicial moralism', offering the Ladies Directory case, *Shaw* v *Director of Public Prosecutions* [1962], as an example of the House of Lords resurrecting the old common law offence of conspiracy to corrupt public morals. Against Hart's 'separability thesis' (which demands the separation of legal from moral considerations – see page 85), this offence had not been used since the nineteenth century (and was also applied in *Knuller* v *Director of Public Prosecutions* [1972]) and was understood to signal the judiciary's sympathy with Devlin's attempt to enforce society's 'moral values'. Hart said this was a high price to pay in sacrificing 'the principle of legality which requires criminal offences to be as precisely defined as possible, so that it can be known with reasonable certainty beforehand what acts are criminal and what are not'.

Ronald Dworkin recommends abandonment of the Hart–Devlin debate and focus on the distinction between general and basic liberties. General liberties 'are derived from an abstract general right to equality, the right to be treated by the government with equal concern and respect' and protect everyone's general right to achieve particular goals. People have interests beyond general liberties and these basic liberties allow the exercise of 'the right of moral independence', where consenting adults can order their own moral priorities, which may include indulging in sadomasochistic play, as in the so-called 'Operation Spanner case', *R* v *Brown* [1994] 1 AC 212.

Be critical

You could critique the idea that some legal theorists believe that the application of J.S. Mill's harm principle can only be defended where harm is likely to other people or property, but cannot apply to ourselves and our own property. If you live alone in the Sahara Desert and feel like burning down your yurt, clearly only you will suffer loss and harm; if, however, you live in Scunthorpe and decide you don't like your apartment, burning it down will evidently harm other people and their property. We live in an individualistic society and the question as to the rightful legal enforcement of public standards of morality in private contexts remains pertinent and an on-going lively area of debate. Think about some of those modern contexts (for example, extreme body piercing, sado-masochism, prostitution and even the work of controversial public artists such as Damien Hirst) and how legal theory informs how such practices are viewed and the legal boundaries fixed accordingly.

■ Putting it all together

Answer guidelines

See the sample question at the start of the chapter.

Approaching the question

This rhetorical question arises out of the *Hart* v *Devlin* debate. It relates to the recommendations of the Wolfenden Report against which Devlin argued, rejecting the idea of a sphere of private morality. He insisted that society depends upon a shared public morality and that it, therefore, has a right to make laws that both protect and defend that morality. Your essay will discuss the key debates within jurisprudence that contextualise the arguments for and against a set of moral criteria with which to evaluate the rightful content of legislation and sanctioning of actions carried out in private. By consideration of key cases in the area of private rights and morality (these may encompass such issues as abortion, assisted dying and body-piercing), you will explore and critically evaluate any shift between moderate and extreme judicial positions on the enforcement of morality in their deliberations and final decisions.

Important points to include

Make sure you are familiar with and include:

- The reasons why the question of the separation of law and morals is important
- The *Hart* v *Fuller* debate
- Fuller's 'inner morality of law'
- The *Hart* v *Devlin* debate and the significance of the Wolfenden Report
- Devlin's 'right-thinking person'
- J.S. Mill's 'harm principle'
- Case law examples that illustrate the judiciary's stance on the private v. public morality divide – for example, contrast the decisions in *R* v *Brown* [1994] 1 AC 212, *R* v *Wilson* [1996] 2 Cr App Rep 241, *Laskey, Jaggard and Brown* v *UK* [1997] 24 EHRR 3, *R* v *Aitken and Others* [1992] 1 WLR 1066 and *R* v *Jones* [1987] Crim LR 123.

Make your answer stand out

There is a good deal of argument made forcefully for and against the consideration of morality in law, and it is tempting to describe these legal positions with a few case examples, or even by referring to the fictional *Speluncean Explorers*, without contrasting these diverse viewpoints. Be sure, however, to make key comparisons between these competing positions and, where appropriate, refer to the fundamental moral issue or debate that has been a major catalyst in shaping the law. One good example is the Wolfenden Report and the effect its vigorous discussion has had on legal innovations relating to homosexuality. Remember to also mention the limitations of such debate in relation to private v. public morality – for example, the law recognises many same-sex rights but does not extend a liberal attitude to sado-masochistic practices or the right of a post-operative transsexual to have their biological child's birth certificate changed retrospectively to reflect the father's gender reassignment; *JK, R (on the application of)* v *Secretary of State for the Home Department & Another* [2015] EWHC 990 (Admin). This is a large area, on which there are many legal theories and opinions, so pick out what you believe to be the main positions that characterise this important area, and be sure to support these with a couple of contrasting key cases.

READ TO IMPRESS

Beyleveld, D. and Brownsword, R. (1986) *Law as a Moral Judgement*. London: Sweet & Maxwell, 326–356.

Dyzenhaus, D. (2008) The Hart–Fuller Debate at Fifty: the grudge informer case revisited. *New York University Law Review*, 83: 1000–1034.

Fuller, L.L. (1949) The Case of the Speluncean Explorers. *Harvard Law Review*, 62: 616–645.

Fuller, L.L. (2007) Positivism and Fidelity to the Law – A reply to Professor Hart, in *Law and Morality: Readings in Legal Philosophy*, 3rd edition. D. Dyzenhaus, S. Moreau and A. Ripstein (eds). Toronto: University of Toronto Press, 67–107.

Kramer, M.H. (2008) *Where Law and Morality Meet*. Oxford: Oxford University Press, 76–102.

Lacey, N. (2008) Philosophy, Political Morality, and History: Explaining the Enduring Resonance of the Hart-Fuller Debate. *New York University Law Review*, 83: 1059–1087.

MacCormick, N. (2008) Judging: Legal cases and moral questions, in *Practical Reason in Law and Morality (Law, State, and Practical Reason)*. Oxford: Oxford University Press, 171–192.

McBride, N.J. and Steel, S. (2014) The Morality of Legality, in *Great Debates in Jurisprudence*. London: Palgrave Macmillan, 66–81.

Norrie, A. (2005) *Law and the Beautiful Soul*. London: Glasshouse Press, Routledge-Cavendish, 53–74.

Simmonds, N.E. (2007) *Law as a Moral Idea*. Oxford: Oxford University Press, 1–36.

www.pearsoned.co.uk/lawexpress

Go online to access more revision support, including quizzes to test your knowledge, sample questions with answer guidelines, podcasts you can download and more!

Classical and modern natural law

4

Revision checklist

Essential points you should know:

☐ What is natural law or the law of nature?

☐ The classical origins of natural law

☐ Key classical natural law theories of the Ancient Greeks and Romans (Aristotle, Plato, Cicero and the Stoics as well as Thomas Aquinas)

☐ Key modern natural law theories of Immanuel Kant, Lon Fuller and John Finnis

☐ The relationship between natural law and legal positivism

■ Topic map

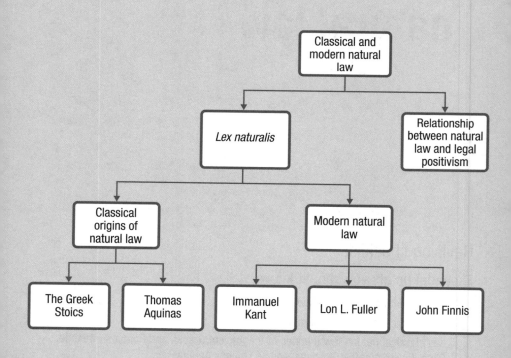

◼ Introduction

Lex naturalis: defining natural law or the law of nature

From the time of the Ancient Greek civilisation, around 3000 BC, natural law has been a constant influence in legal and ethical thinking. Its early appeal was fundamentally of a religious nature, whilst later periods have witnessed natural law used as a moral justification in legal, social and political contexts. It has the unquestionable aura of the sacred and is often presented as a higher form of law – determining not only what the law *is* but, by the application of reason, inferring what the law *ought* to be. Lawyers and academics continue to disagree about where to fix the boundaries relating to the precise content of natural law. As a general proposition, it can be agreed that, following from an understanding of human nature and human capacities, natural law theory offers a critical account of what constitutes well-being and fulfilment both for individuals and society. To this end, theories of natural law address the grounds and content of our moral obligations by indicating how we might identify the principles of right action, namely moral principles, which urge people to act in accordance with the common good. Some natural lawyers also assume that the legitimate aim of any legal system is to secure justice. They believe that, notwithstanding the legitimacy of law-making powers, there is an obligation not to make unjust laws; as Cicero stated '*lex iniusta non est lex*' or 'an unjust law is not law'. Similarly, Aquinas held that laws that conform only to the appearance of laws are nothing more than a 'perversion of law'; only law derived from natural law (by the application of human reason, which gives it a moral dimension) is capable of determining just law, which commands our obedience.

Modern natural law theory has evidenced a shift from the idea of 'natural right' to 'natural rights'. John Finnis constructs his theory of natural law around the idea of a common pursuit of basic goods towards which all persons feel an entitlement. Whilst the attainment of such goods provides a reason for action, the principle of morality dictates that one ought to make choices and act in a way that is compatible only with integral human fulfilment, towards benefitting others as well as oneself. The idea of universality, equal treatment and respect owed to all human beings (by virtue of their humanity) is not only the master principle of morality but also a primary principle of human rights, which is also at the core of most modern natural law theories. To summarise, natural law theories propose to identify moral principles of right action that others have a duty to respect and governments are compelled not only to respect but, to the greatest extent possible, also to protect.

ASSESSMENT ADVICE

An essay or examination question will mostly likely assume you understand why natural law standards, according to which the law *ought* to be judged, are commonly referred to as those of a 'higher law'. You can explain this claim as originating in a *literal* understanding, which refers to the classical origins of divine-inspired or religious-text-based natural law and law founded upon (or at least supported by) human reason. Alternatively, a *metaphorical* explanation would suggest that the higher law epithet relates to the connection to the moral status of law; that to merit our obedience, law must appeal to an intrinsic moral justification – which should not be ignored when determining the right choice or action. You will be expected to offer examples of legal theories that represent these positions.

■ Sample question

Could you answer this question? Below is a typical essay question that could arise on this topic. Guidelines on answering the question are included at the end of this chapter. Another sample question and guidance on tackling it can be found on the companion website.

ESSAY QUESTION

'The concern of the [natural law] tradition … has been to show that the act of "positing" law (whether judicially or legislatively or otherwise) is an act which can and should be guided by "moral" principles and rules; that those moral norms are a matter of objective reasonableness, not of whim, convention, or mere "decision".' – Finnis, *Natural Law and Natural Rights*.

Discuss, by reference to key legal theories, the modern relevance of natural law.

■ The classical origins of natural law

The origins of natural law are obscure, but we can appreciate the influence of classical moral philosophy on the development of key principles. Justinian's sixth-century *Digest* records the classical Roman jurist Ulpian relating the term 'law' to four elements: art, religion, ethics and philosophy, and describes the learning of law as the 'knowledge of things divine and human, and the science of what is just or unjust'. Because of their calling to cultivate justice and acquire knowledge of right and wrong, he likened lawyers to priests who were similarly well-versed in the art (not the mechanical application) of the good and equitable. The flexibility of Roman law meant that any settled rules and principles had to be interpreted in the light of equity and particular circumstances. Lawyers needed to use their skill to make compromises in taking account of competing aims in authoritative texts rather than rigidly following settled rules and procedures. In the cause of justice, moral principles were held to be capable of explaining legal rules and deciding contested legal issues, as these can be derived from the innate human capacities of intelligence and reason.

The law of nature, or natural law, was understood by the Romans as rational (comprehensible by natural reason) and allowed for justifications to be given for obeying or disobeying rules and institutions. Their conception of natural law, therefore, offered the possibility of self-defence; ruling out any obligation to perform what was by nature deemed impossible. Since society is made up of people who are meant to live together, it was considered wrong to impede the development and exercise of one's own innate capacities and those of others. In this way, early natural law was also closely connected to the idea of restraint and respect for others.

Aristotle, Plato and, three-quarters of a century later, Roman lawyer, philosopher and statesman Cicero, were all early exponents of natural law, which the latter described as the 'true' law. Influenced by the Stoics, Cicero suggested three distinguishing features of natural law: (1) it is a manifestation of the Divine will and is consequently universal, eternal and unalterable; (2) its rules must be discovered through the application of reason; and (3) all persons are obliged to obey these rules. Any breach constitutes a violation of one's true nature, which is punishment enough as the 'abandonment of his better self' means a person can no longer live in a state of peaceful harmony or justice. This early conception of natural law determines moral principles to be immanent in nature and they alone can direct our actions. Beyond such generalisations, natural law theories are diverse and the core conceptions are introduced below.

◼ The Stoics and natural law

KEY THEORIST

The Stoics

Arguably the most important philosophy in Rome was Stoicism, which originated in Hellenistic Greece. The Stoic legacy has been instrumental in setting out the basis for early natural law. Essentially following the logic of Aristotle, the Stoics believed in a world governed by chance and necessity, free from divine or human interference, leaving humans in a state of nature. In this non-hierarchical world of possibility, the origin of knowledge and criterion of truth (accessed by the mind through the senses) could only be attained by reason, which was considered to be an innate ability, common to all people.

The Stoic definition of morality, in agreement with Plato and Aristotle, was synonymous with a life lived (against whim and self-will, rather) according to reason. As virtue was considered to be grounded on reason and therefore knowledge, the wise person (familiar with, for example, science, logic and physics) was equated with the good person whose conduct accords with good rather than foolish or evil principles. Every human being was considered to be capable of obedience to the law of nature; in other words, to quote Immanuel Kant from his *Critique of Practical Reason*, governed by 'the starry skies above me and the moral law within me'.

■ The importance of Aquinas' natural law theory

KEY THEORIST

Thomas Aquinas (1225–1274)

St Thomas Aquinas was a thirteenth-century theologian and philosopher whose seminal work, *Summa Theologica*, still exerts a profound influence on modern natural law theorists. At the core of his natural law theory is the claim that moral standards, and consequently moral law, are derived from the nature of the world and human beings within it; and so natural law is 'an ordinance of reason'. Made in God's image, human beings have the capacity of reason, which enables them to be able to deduce right actions towards the 'common good'.

William Blackstone, in his *Commentaries on the Law of England*, states that since **Aquinas' natural law theory** is 'dictated by God' and is consequently considered 'superior in obligation to any other ... binding over all the globe, in all countries, and at all times: no human laws are of any validity, if contrary to this; and such of them as are valid derive all their force, and all their authority from this original'. Laws that conflict with the demands of natural law consequently lose their power to bind morally. It is clear, therefore, that laws must be reasonable (if contrary to reason then they cannot qualify as laws), and they must also be directed towards the common good, and not serve the private interests of a few individuals. This means that a government that abuses its authority by enacting unjust laws (laws that are against the common good or unreasonable) lacks moral authority and surrenders any right to obedience.

Aquinas further described reason as the 'rule and measure' in deriving what are 'the first principles' of human actions. Only first principles of natural law, such as 'do no harm', are immutable; deductions from first principles (in other words, secondary principles) can vary under exceptional circumstances. We are not told specifically which principles are designated 'primary', neither are we given any clue as to how secondary principles are derived from primary principles. For Aquinas, however, given that human beings are governed by reason (the faculty common to all), it is morally appropriate that they would conduct themselves in a way that conforms to their rational nature. In this way, Aquinas derives the moral law from the nature of human beings, which constitutes natural law.

KEY DEFINITION: Aquinas' nature of law

Aquinas divided natural law into four distinct types:

- *Lex Aeterna* (Eternal Law): timeless laws that apply to the 'whole community of the universe' and are governed by God, including physical (scientific, biological, etc.) laws as well as God's plan for the universe – without which people would lack direction;

- *Lex Divina* (Divine Law): law revealed by scripture and divine revelation and not by human reason;

- *Lex Naturalis* (Natural Law): that part of eternal law (governing rational behaviour and free will) that is discoverable by reason; the first precept of natural law derives from one's rational nature directed towards avoiding evil and only doing good, which are considered to be both universal and objective aims;

- *Lex Humana* (Human Law): supported by human reason and articulated via human authorities for the common good; a human law is only valid if it conforms to the content or general principles of natural law.

The significance of Kant's rational theory of law

KEY THEORIST

Immanuel Kant (1724–1804)

Kant was a distinguished enlightenment thinker who was influenced by the Ancient Greeks, Aquinas and social contractarians such as Rousseau. Kant's critical theory is founded on the concept of freedom and moral obligation, and the various requirements and duties that these place on ethical behaviour. He argued that any rule we follow must be able to be applied universally; accordingly deontological concerns such as differentiating between the categories of prohibited, mandatory and permissible actions were central to the Kantian project.

Human understanding, for Kant, is the source of the general laws of nature that shape all experience, whilst human reason is able to elucidate the moral law. This means scientific intelligence and morality are mutually consistent, especially since they have the same basis in human agency as rational and moral autonomy, both of which Kant describes as, respectively, the 'ultimate' and 'final' *ends* of nature. In other words, a human has the unique capacity to 'form a concept of ends for himself, and by means of his reason can make a system of ends out of an aggregate of purposively formed things' as 'only a rational being has the capacity of acting according to the conception of laws, that is, according to principles'.

Individuals are not merely privileged by virtue of their natural abilities; rather each person is obliged to seek the 'highest good' and exercise their rational capacities for moral action. For Kant, natural law means that each individual has the freedom, in other words the autonomy, to pursue aims consistent with the moral law (which is both universal and necessary) and must be prescribed by reason alone. The duty to formulate unconditional moral laws, as an autonomous rational agent, was understood by Kant as a non-empirical experience – namely, not to be directed by any personal aims or desires. He referred to this duty as the categorical moral imperative.

 Make your answer stand out

You can explain how natural law theories, such as those of Aquinas and Kant, are often regarded as deontological because, unlike consequentialism (which purports that choices that inform our actions or intentions are morally evaluated solely by the end results), deontological theories propose that all choices must conform to an objective moral norm. For deontologists, like many natural law theorists, the right reason for an action is of paramount importance, and such a moral motivation is completely separated from any consequences. You could provide an example, such as: if to tell lies is morally wrong, then lying is without exception always immoral. Even if the lie protects others (for example, hiding Jews from the Nazis) and so could be morally justified, it would still be viewed by deontologists as morally wrong. Deontological moral systems typically determine the origins of moral duty as divine law or, in the case of Kant, the basis of a categorical imperative that is always morally valid.

KEY DEFINITION: Kant's categorical moral imperative

Kant's categorical moral imperative comprises three important principles; the latter principle combines the first two:

- *Universal Law formulation:* An individual has a duty to act only on moral rules that he would be willing to impose on anyone else; therefore, moral acts of obligation must be capable of universal application (without contradiction).

- *Humanity or End-in-Itself formulation:* Always treat others as ends and not means; to treat other people as ends requires respecting each person as an autonomous rational moral agent with their own aspirations, goals and projects.

- *Kingdom of Ends formulation:* Every rational being must so act as if he were, through his maxim, always a legislating member in the universal kingdom of ends.

The second formulation of Kant's categorical imperative (insisting that we treat other people as ends and never as a means) is considered to be his version of the 'Golden Rule'. His argument for privileging human reason as the source of moral rules and duties rests on two grounds: (1) humans are capable of reason and (2) humans have an independent or autonomous will. On this basis, according to Kant, individuals are able to be self-governing and act as self-legislators, and so they collectively comprise a 'kingdom of ends'. To use other people as a means to our own ends would, therefore, violate their autonomous reason and free will.

■ Fuller's inner morality of law

KEY THEORIST

Lon L. Fuller (1902–1978)

For Lon Fuller, law is a purposive occupation that aspires towards the legal–moral ideal of legality (comprising certain valued procedural principles, commonly associated with the rule of law). He departs from any earlier theological or contemporary rationalist doctrines of natural law or ideas of absolute values, and views the natural law project as a search for the principles of social order. Fuller believes the purpose of law is to 'subject human conduct to the governance of rules' and, to this end, he proposes a formulation of eight principles. These measures are referred to as the 'inner morality of law' and aim to ensure that law-making adheres to a minimum standard.

Fuller treats natural law as a 'collaborative articulation of shared purposes' by which people can come to better 'understand their own ends' and the 'means for achieving them'; and so the 'process of moral discovery is a social one'. A legal system is, therefore, a human enterprise and it is important to strive for 'legal excellence'. Fuller holds that there is a necessary connection between law and morality, but this is founded on a non-dogmatic 'morality of aspiration', which he distinguishes from a 'morality of duty'. For example, a rule that forbids killing may be equally expressed as a duty to respect life, which, in being less prescriptive, allows for a judgement of degree. Fuller's theory is often referred to as a procedural natural law theory because it combines the formal facets of a legal system; and his 1964 *The Morality of Law* orders these facets into eight principles of legality comprising an 'inner morality of law' (discussed in Chapter 3). This set of requirements simply comprises eight general moral rules of duty, which specify the aspiration (and obligation) to treat people, with fairness and justice, as fully equal 'responsible' autonomous agents. Compliance with these measures is argued by Fuller to lead to substantively just laws and would provide a guarantee against bad or evil laws.

Be critical

You could refer to Hart's famous critique of Fuller (from his 1983 *Essays in Jurisprudence and Philosophy*), in which he insists that *The Morality of Law* is an essentially content-free formulation, as Fuller does not outline any substantive moral values that must be met by law. Hart further claims these eight measures are merely 'principles of efficacy' and it is absurd to refer to them as 'moral' any more than the 'inner morality of poisoning' – as clear laws could also further evil ends. You could, in turn, critique Hart on the basis that he misunderstands Fuller's central point, which is 'fidelity to the law', and the central idea that 'evil laws' lack logic, coherence and consistency – which are key factors in his eight principles.

For Fuller, law is the 'enterprise of subjecting human conduct to the governance of rules'; this means it is important that the application of these principles allows individuals to understand the scope of legal rules and therefore influence their practical reasoning towards right actions – as they should be able to speculate how the judiciary may interpret such rules and may be aware of possible punishments for any breach. As long as total failure with regard to any one principle is avoided, law-makers can meet the requirements of the rule of law to a varying extent and still succeed in making law. This is an important consideration, since when law-makers fall short of the ideal of legality and expectations are ambiguous or contradictory, people feel resentment as they are being judged according to a standard that they were given no reasonable opportunity to meet. The requirement that laws be general, clear and predictable (therefore ensuring a moral obligation of obedience) emphasises the essential partnership between legislator and subject, having a joint interest in the formulation of substantively just laws.

■ Finnis' natural law theory and the principle of practical reasonableness

KEY THEORIST

John Finnis (b. 1940)

John Finnis' natural law theory emulates the original ideology of Aquinas, in as much as he also claims that normative propositions about what law *ought* to be are not derived (as positivist critics of natural law claim) from a bare description of the natural world of what *is*. His 1980 book, *Natural Law and Natural Rights*, appeals to the distinctive moral aim of the 'common good' and how best to order social interaction towards this purpose. Against the positivist agenda, Finnis further suggests that any attempt to explain the law in objective terms fails, as it necessarily makes assumptions about what is good.

FINNIS' NATURAL LAW THEORY AND THE PRINCIPLE OF PRACTICAL REASONABLENESS

Unlike Aquinas, Finnis does not base his theory on theology, rather he insists that natural laws do not originate from anything; they are simply 'self-evident' and founded on the fact that humans have a common need for certain 'basic goods'. Finnis rejects both Hume's idea of practical reason (which can only tell us how to best achieve our desires) and Aquinas' first principle of practical reason, which similarly emphasises how good is to be sought and evil avoided. The emphasis for Finnis is not so much on how goods are sought in order to promote true human flourishing, rather he adopts an Aristotelian approach in defining what ought to be the proper object(s) of our desire for a good life. Along with general notions that commonly comprise any theory of justice, such as equality, freedom and fairness, Finnis elucidates a further layer of seven essential basic goods or values (those which all rational actors would want for themselves – see KEY DEFINITION: **Finnis' 7 basic goods**). Since individuals must often choose how to balance such goods with one another, simply recognising the goods is not sufficient to assimilate them into true human flourishing. There are no overriding or metaphysical principles that can resolve all disagreements, and Finnis is keen to avoid a **teleology** or specified hierarchy of values. Rather, in order to achieve those basic goods, he determines that moral and legal rules must be enacted that meet the standards of practical reasonableness.

The requirements of practical reasonableness are set out in nine basic principles; these comprise the 'natural law method' of working out what is the moral 'natural law' from the first (pre-moral) list of seven 'basic forms of human flourishing'. Together these make up the universal and immutable 'principles of natural law' (see KEY DEFINITION: **Finnis' 9 basic requirements of practical reasonableness**). Practical reason is the starting point for an individual, in considering the ways in which human flourishing for oneself and others can be promoted and protected, balancing our pursuit of these goods against a wider societal interest – which requires both fairness and foresight. Finnis suggests practical reasonableness rests on the premise that there is a general inclination, a 'united directedness', towards promoting the well-being of others; which echoes certain aspects of Kant's doctrine of the moral law as set out in his 1788 *Critique of Practical Reason* and 1797 *The Metaphysics of Morals*. Legal authority is considered to be legitimate when derived from the natural law, as based on unchanging principles that acquire their force from the principle of reasonableness and not from any originating acts or circumstances. The foundation of legal authority rests, therefore, on the likelihood of compliance. It is further recognised that the desirability of authority as a means of obtaining the common good is a presumptively adequate basis for recognising (and complying) with a rationally formulated positive legal rule as valid legislation. For Finnis, therefore, natural law offers a rational basis for the determination of positive law in addition to a set of criteria for individual judgement as to whether or not a law merits our obedience.

KEY DEFINITION: Finnis' 7 basic goods

Finnis has outlined seven basic goods, which motivate all human endeavour and are fundamental to all human life. They are not listed hierarchically, nor do they derive from other goods, and are irreducible to other things. The first three are *substantive*, which means they exist prior to action, and the remaining four are *reflexive*, which means they depend on the choices we make:

- *Life and health*: related to the idea of self-preservation;
- *Knowledge*: for its own sake, not merely instrumental, and related to the idea of curiosity;
- *Play*: 'which [has] no point beyond the performance itself';
- *Aesthetic experience*: the appreciation of beauty;
- *Sociability and friendship*: 'acting for the sake of one's friend's purposes, one's friend's well-being';
- *Practical reasonableness*: 'the basic good of being able to bring one's own intelligence to bear effectively … on the problems of choosing one's actions and life-style and shaping one's own character';
- *Religion*: a general concern for the order of the cosmos, human freedom and reason.

KEY DEFINITION: Finnis' 9 basic requirements of practical reasonableness

The following nine methodological requirements of practical reasonableness are claimed by Finnis to enable us to make decisions about how to act, what basic goods to choose and generally how to order our lives. They are also purported to be fundamental to the concept of natural law:

- Harmony of purpose/a coherent plan of life
- No arbitrary preferences amongst values
- No arbitrary preferences amongst persons
- Detachment from particular realisations of good (avoiding fanaticism)
- Fidelity to commitments (avoiding apathy and/or fickleness)
- Efficacy (within limits)
- Respect for every basic value
- Respect for community and the common good
- Following one's conscience and being authentic.

■ The relationship between natural law and legal positivism

The entire chronicle of the philosophy of law can be summarised as an endless argument between two major theories (or collections of theories) – legal positivism and natural law theory, comprising two disparate attitudes towards how law should be evaluated. In general, the theories characteristic of legal positivism can be seen to have emerged as a reaction – within a particular historical period – to natural law, which has its origins in early Greek philosophy. Based on different and irreconcilable concepts of the law, the unresolved discord turns mainly on their differing assumptions about the relationship between law and morality. Whilst positivism is concerned with what lawyers actually say and do in order to identify and explain the concept of law, natural lawyers rely on the capacity of human nature to tell us what *ought* to be done – emphasising the ethical necessity of law.

Legal positivism, therefore, seeks to formally identify positive legal rules, in order to articulate a minimum framework for social order and legitimise state authority in its ability to impose regulations and apply sanctions. Procedural efficacy is a chief concern. Consequently, legal positivists are often critical of natural law theory's propensity to connect law with human good, as well as their refusal to answer the question of whether something is or is not law. Natural law theorists are more concerned with identifying the limits of the right of legal institutions to make laws, and the nature and limitations of any obligation to the law – so the quality and appropriateness of law-making is of chief concern. Significantly for natural lawyers, the basis of law is said to be found in human nature and, as such, the ideal of law is historical, universal and immutable – it cannot be changed by human intervention alone.

📖 **REVISION NOTE**

Be sure to revise not only the key players in natural law theory but also their critics, and be familiar with the general basis for any criticisms. Look up unfamiliar terms and become accustomed to using these in context, such as *deontological ethics*. You will also need to remember the various formulae that attach to particular theories, such as examples from Finnis' 7 basic goods, so you can explain their significance and why it is necessary to attach these to his 9 basic requirements of practical reasonableness.

Be critical

Natural law theorists hold that moral appraisal is absolutely integral to describing and analysing legal rules. This is repudiated by those within the legal positivist tradition, who insist that the only proper approach to identifying legal rules is by being morally neutral. As well as such fundamental areas of disagreement, there is some evidence of almost-shared ground on certain positions between contemporary legal theorists on opposite sides of the divide. Raz, a modern legal positivist, concedes that law 'purports to' generate moral grounds for action, whilst Finnis holds that law 'does' actually generate moral grounds for action under certain circumstances. Although still adopting different positions, the difference is not so marked as between, say, Austin and Aquinas. Bear in mind this sort of nuanced reasoning when setting out your approach to an assignment or exam question on this topic.

■ Putting it all together

Answer guidelines

See the sample question at the start of the chapter.

Approaching the question

The question leads with a quotation from Finnis, a contemporary natural lawyer, who is here making two claims. First of all, he associates law-making with necessary moral considerations and, secondly, suggests these are only discoverable by reason. The quotation offers an updated view of natural law; however, it also provides a basis for discussing the general tenets of natural law theory, so you could address the relevance of natural law by briefly discussing the evolution of natural law (from its discovery by the Stoics to modern theories) in relation to the continuing centrality of moral reasoning and the shift from divine to human reason. You might then posit some of the kind of questions natural lawyers ask of the law-making process, and how they relate to their big idea of the wider 'ethical' purpose of the government and legal institutions.

Law is concerned not only with the achievement of obedience, but also with the 'duty' to obey. The idea that individuals are able to choose for themselves (by virtue of their 'humanity' and capacity for reason) the right 'moral' principles for action is also unique to natural lawyers and has been finessed over time by various theorists. As for whether the ideas and claims of natural lawyers are relevant to the conditions of our existence in the modern world, the same issues relating to (a) the fixing of moral–legal normative standards (e.g., civil partnerships, human embryo research), (b) the relationship of law to 'justice' and (c) questions of legitimacy remain contentious areas of legal inquiry to which there are no simple, or scientific, solutions.

Important points to include

■ Natural law theories act as reflective critical accounts of the constitutive aspects of the well-being and flourishing of individuals and the communities they form.

■ The propositions that select fundamental aspects of human flourishing provide more than merely instrumental motivations for action and self-restraint. They are directive, or prescriptive, in our thinking about what we ought and ought not to do; the product of our practical reason.

■ Theories of natural law seek to identify principles for right action – in other words, moral principles.

■ Every person seeks their own fulfilment, according to their human nature. The first (and most general) principle of morality, however, is that individuals should always choose to act in a manner that is compatible with a will towards integral human well-being or the 'common good'.

■ Amongst such principles is a respect for the rights people possess simply by virtue of their humanity. These are rights that, as a matter of justice, others are obliged to respect and governments are compelled not only to respect but also to protect.

■ Natural law has been refined through centuries of reflection, continuing to the present day. Modern legal theorists, such as Finnis, attest to the possibility of a morally just legal system that orders civil society by working for the common good.

 Make your answer stand out

It would be a good idea to mention that by reflecting on the basic goods of human nature (especially those most immediately relevant to social and political life), natural law theorists propose to develop a comprehensive understanding of the principles of justice, including those principles we refer to as human rights. You could explain how accounts of practical reasoning and moral judgement can provide or justify the basis of positive law in addition to offering standards for its critical appraisal. Refer to supporting sources such as Beyleveld and Brownsword's 1986 *Law as a Moral Judgement* (see Chapter 3), which asserts that judgement is essentially a moral exercise that will, over time, realise its natural purpose (namely, a moral purpose) towards doing what is right and in the interests of the common good. There is a wide variety of other modern theories that can support your arguments: for example, look for recent journal articles and book chapters written by Alan Gewirth, Robert George and Mark Murphy.

READ TO IMPRESS

Finnis, J. (2002) Natural Law: The Classical Tradition, in *The Oxford Handbook of Jurisprudence and Philosophy of Law*. J. Coleman and S. Shapiro (eds). Oxford: Oxford University Press, 1–60.

Fuller, L.L. (2007) Positivism and Fidelity to the Law – A reply to Professor Hart, in *Law and Morality: Readings in Legal Philosophy*, 3rd edition. D. Dyzenhaus, S. Moreau and A. Ripstein (eds). Toronto: University of Toronto Press, 67–107.

Gardner, J. (2007) Nearly Natural Law. *American Journal of Jurisprudence*, 52: 1–23.

George, R.P. (2008) Natural Law. *Harvard Journal of Law & Public Policy*, 31(1): 171–196.

Gewirth, A. (1984) The Ontological Basis of Natural Law: A Critique and an Alternative. *American Journal of Jurisprudence*, 29(1): 95–121.

Manderson, D. (2010) HLA Hart, Lon Fuller and the Ghosts of Legal Interpretation. *Windsor Yearbook of Access to Justice*, 28(1): 81–110.

Murphy, C. (2005) Lon Fuller and the Moral Value of the Rule of Law. *Law and Philosophy*, 24: 239–262.

Murphy, M.C. (2003) *Natural Law in Jurisprudence and Politics*. Cambridge: Cambridge University Press, 1–24.

Nobles, R. and Schiff, D. (2005) *Introduction to Jurisprudence and Legal Theory: Commentary and Materials*. J. Penner, D. Schiff and R. Nobles (eds). Oxford: Oxford University Press, 35–90.

Raz, J. (2004) Incorporation by Law. *Legal Theory*, 10: 1–17.

Wacks, R. (2015) *Understanding Jurisprudence: An Introduction to Legal Theory*, 4th edition. Oxford: Oxford University Press, 14–48.

www.pearsoned.co.uk/lawexpress

 Go online to access more revision support, including quizzes to test your knowledge, sample questions with answer guidelines, podcasts you can download and more!

Classical and modern legal positivism

Revision checklist

Essential points you should know:

- [ ] The significance of legal positivism: the 'ruling theory of law'
- [ ] Separating the *is* and *ought* of legal positivism: asking the morality question
- [ ] Introducing H.L.A. Hart's central principles of legal positivism
- [ ] Key classical legal positivists: Jeremy Bentham and John Austin
- [ ] Key modern legal positivists: Hans Kelsen, H.L.A. Hart and Joseph Raz
- [ ] Ronal Dworkin's influential anti-positivist theory
- [ ] The significance of the *Hart* v *Dworkin* debate: a critique of legal positivism

Topic map

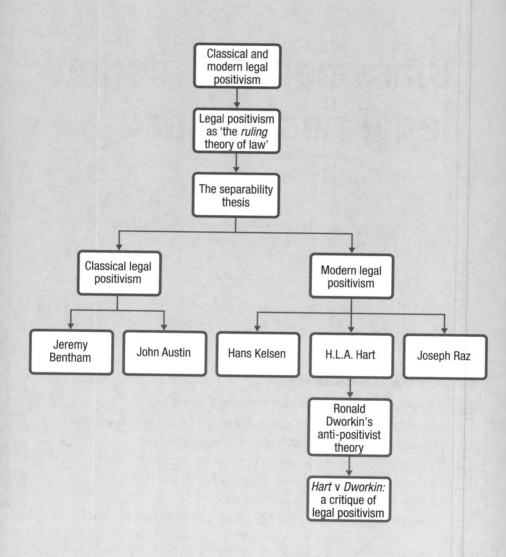

■ Introduction

Legal positivism: 'the ruling theory of law'

In *Taking Rights Seriously* Ronald Dworkin describes an ideal theory of law as a 'complete legal theory', namely one that tells us both what the law *is* and what it *ought* to be. Dworkin further claims that legal positivism as the prevailing or 'ruling theory of law' attends only to the former premise, by adopting a descriptive and, importantly, morally neutral hypothesis about the nature of law. Critics of this dominant theory further assert that the conception of natural rights is rejected, and any moral content and criteria relating to considerations of legality, legitimacy or legal validation are to be excluded. This is because, for legal positivists, the existence of law is not dependent on ideals of justice or even the abstract rule of law; rather, law and legal institutions are presented as a simple matter of social fact.

Legal positivists suggest that law, properly directed, is not dedicated to the interests it *ought* to serve, rather to those it must serve from a practical and procedural point of view. Official recognition of the various processes and standards of various authoritative systems of governance, such as law courts, legislative enactments and social conventions, determines law's clarity and continuing existence. As characterised by a dependency on a set of explicitly adopted rules, it is largely taken for granted that this relatively uncomplicated approach to law is the preferred working philosophy of most practising lawyers.

ASSESSMENT ADVICE

Essay and examination questions will require you to explain why legal positivists insist on the separation of law and morals, and to put forward the variant interpretations of key legal theorists on this topic – comparing the views of, for example, Austin, Bentham, Kelsen and Hart. You will also be expected to be able to critically evaluate core concepts such as Hart's 'rule of recognition', Austin's 'command theory' and Kelsen's '*grundnorm*', since such concepts are characteristic of the positivist project and give substance to their claims of a scientifically grounded, non-moral and socially constructed system of law.

■ Sample question

Could you answer this question? Below is a typical essay question that could arise on this topic. Guidelines on answering the question are included at the end of this chapter. Another sample question and guidance on tackling it can be found on the companion website.

Moral values have arguably influenced the content of certain laws, such as those relating to civil partnerships and abortion. Is it desirable, or even possible, to make law without reference to a moral objective or moral reference point? Discuss in relation to those views expressed by key legal philosophers from within the positivist tradition.

■ Separating the '*is*' and the '*ought*' of legal positivism

Although it is important not to confuse the general with the particular, it is held by most classical legal positivists that issues of legal validity are to be strictly separated from questions of morality, since it is claimed there is no requirement that law satisfy moral demands. The '*separability thesis*' is rigorously defended by modern legal positivist H.L.A. Hart, to articulate the claim that there is no 'necessary' connection between law and morality, and generally speaking all varieties of legal positivism can be defined by their commitment to this idea.

The validity of a legal norm is established on the basis of its provenance and not its moral correctness, so there is no necessary or logical relationship between what the law *is* and what the law *ought* to be. According to Austin, in his 1832 *The Province of Jurisprudence Determined*, the 'existence of law is one thing; its merit or demerit is another. Whether it be or be not is one enquiry; whether it be or be not conformable to an assumed standard, is a different enquiry. A law, which actually exists, is a law, though we happen to dislike it, or though it may vary from the text by which we regulate our approbation and disapprobation.' For example, since a murderer fails to give weight to their moral obligation not to murder, it is unlikely they will acknowledge a moral duty to obey the law of murder. Only the threat of sanction is an effective deterrent. Consequently, legal positivism conceives and structures law according to a set of formal criteria that have no need for either a moral or ethical foundation.

Early Roman author Tertullian affirmed the central ordering concept of 'command', 'It is our duty to obey a demand of God [or the state], not because it is just but because it has been issued by God', so then the sovereign decree obviates the need for legitimation by any higher moral principle. The corollary of this assertion is that a law can be perceived as unjust or evil, yet citizens are bound to obey it and officials are entitled to punish any act of defiance. The fear of subjective notions of justice along with the strict prioritisation of legal certainty has resulted in the rigid separation of the *is* and *ought* by many legal positivists, most notably Kelsen in his formulation of a 'pure theory of law'.

KEY DEFINITION: Hart's central tenets of legal positivism

As is the case with regard to any school of jurisprudence, there are wide variations between theorists as to where to fix the boundaries of knowledge and what constitutes the main ideas. H.L.A. Hart attempts to provide a classification of main themes that are characteristic of legal positivism, as set out in his 1983 *Essays in Jurisprudence and Philosophy*:

■ laws are commands of human beings;

■ there is no necessary connection between law and morals, or law as it is and law as it ought to be;

■ the analysis of legal concepts is worth pursuing and is to be distinguished from historical inquiries, from sociological inquiries, and from the criticism or appraisal of law;

■ a legal system is a closed legal system in which correct legal decisions can be deduced by logical means from predetermined legal rules; *Realism? Dworkin?*

■ moral judgements cannot be established or defended, as statements of fact can, by rational argument, evidence or proof.

▧ Main theorists within the tradition of legal positivism

Nineteenth-century legal theorists John Austin and Jeremy Bentham are commonly associated with the development of early or classical legal positivism; more recently, Hans Kelsen followed by H.L.A. Hart and Joseph Raz are credited with the evolution of contemporary legal positivism. You may also come across Thomas Hobbes and David Hume, whose views are said to have influenced Austin and Bentham. For Hume, laws are simply the expression of a changing pattern of social and political interaction, properly explicated on the basis of scientific observation and analysis rather than by an appeal to moral or theological considerations. It follows, therefore, that it is impossible to derive normative claims (how law ought to be) from descriptive claims (how law is); this is one of the fundamental tenets of legal positivism. Often referred to as the forefather of 'empiricist legal positivism', Hobbes – in his seminal 1651 *Leviathan* – identifies law with 'command', defined as 'where a man says, "do this", or "do not do this", without expecting other reason than the will of him that says it'. So then, like Hume, Hobbes considers law to be a matter of empirically discernible social fact underpinned by the dictate of a coercive sovereign authority that commands our respect and, importantly, obedience – without the necessity for moral evaluation. To paraphrase Leo Tolstoy's 1870's *Anna Karenina*, 'All happy legal theorists resemble each other; every unhappy legal theorist is unhappy in their own way.' As is the case with many areas of jurisprudential inquiry, the origins of legal positivism, its core hypotheses and what these represent are contested and continue to be the cause of much disagreement within mainstream legal scholarship.

KEY DEFINITION: Empiricism

Empiricism belongs to **epistemology**, which is concerned with studying the nature, origins and boundaries of knowledge. Empiricists claim that knowledge of the world and its objects is derived from sensory experience and empirical evidence, and can only be known and justified through experience. Concepts based on reason, and intuitive propositions that can be either true or false, are rejected as unreliable since they are not based on observational evidence.

KEY THEORIST

Jeremy Bentham (1748–1832)

Jeremy Bentham formulated one of the most comprehensive theories of classical legal positivism along with a complex language of analysis and a framework of principles with which to think systematically about law; however, much of his work remained unpublished until recent decades. A major impetus was the restructuring of the common law, which he perceived as arbitrary and based on unconnected rules as well as being too susceptible to judicial caprice and creativity, referring derisively to the court system as 'Judge & Co'. His intention was to posit a more accessible and, significantly, man-made basis, far removed from the continental natural law and natural rights movement, which prioritised the cultivation of higher principles rather than the social good. Bentham described natural rights as 'imaginary rights' (rhetorical nonsense or 'nonsense on stilts'), unlike the 'real rights' produced by actual existing systems of law.

Bentham divided jurisprudence into two distinct categories. *Censorial* jurisprudence tells us what law should be and enquires into 'the art of judgement' (in other words, belongs to the normative tradition), whilst *Expository* jurisprudence (the exposition of existing law) expresses what the law is, characteristic of the positivist approach. He further distinguished two types of expository jurisprudence, namely, *authoritative* when expressed by the legislator representing the state and *unauthoritative* when presented by 'any other person at large' or not emanating from a sovereign authority. Therefore, a parental order to their child or an employer's order to an employee can be legal mandates in the same way as a judicial pronouncement. In this way, Bentham extends the remit of positive law to acts and sources outside the context of formal legal practice and instruments, with the important caveat that they each must accord with the will of the sovereign. Addition of this latter category distinguishes him from Austin, who recognised *only* the sovereign as a legitimate source of power. Bentham's revisionary analysis of law introduces the idea of public opinion and social influence alongside the traditional command model; both types have a role to play in elucidating a complete body of laws towards the formation of a 'universal expository jurisprudence'.

KEY THEORY

Utilitarianism

Jeremy Bentham is perhaps most famously known for his utilitarianism, based on the 'greatest happiness' or utility principle (emulated by John Stuart Mill a generation later); it is not to be confused with an ethical principle such as rightness or goodness. Utilitarianism comprises a legal and moral theory in which the attainment of happiness, as the greatest good for the greatest number of people, was considered to be the proper end of human action, as it is nothing more than the aggregate of individual human interests. A socially hedonistic legal system based on the utility principle privileges the goal of happiness (or pleasure) as opposed to pain, and governs not only how human beings act but also how they ought to act. The precept 'a punishment to fit the crime' is a utilitarian principle, in that the punishment of criminals is an effective mode of crime prevention because it alters the likely outcome of their behaviour, attaching the possibility of future pain in order to outweigh any pleasure or gain in committing the crime.

KEY DEFINITION: Consequentialism

Utilitarianism is, by modern legal theorists, considered to be a form of **consequentialism**, which belongs to the branch of **normative ethics** and explores the basis for right or moral actions. Consequentialists maintain that the consequences of human action form the basis for any judgement concerning the rightness of that conduct, so a morally right act (or omission) is one that will produce a good outcome, or consequence.

KEY THEORIST

John Austin (1790–1859)

John Austin takes a simple view of law, and a narrow view of the jurisprudential approach that characterised the evolution of positivism throughout the nineteenth century and well into the twentieth. Austin's more straightforward methodological positivism influenced the development of *analytical jurisprudence*, as opposed to those approaches to law that are based on history or sociology, or complex arguments about law that were secondary to more general moral and political theories. The emphasis of Austin's analytical jurisprudence on key concepts, such as legal right and duty, continued to dominate English legal theory until the emergence of Hart's seminal contribution, discussed below.

5 CLASSICAL AND MODERN LEGAL POSITIVISM

In common with Bentham's classic formulation of the positivist doctrine, for Austin legality is related to the source of a norm, not the merits of its contents. Unlike Bentham's intellectual methodology and approach to legal positivism, however, for Austin law is outlined as uncomplicated and precise. Laws are laid down by 'political superiors to [be followed by] political inferiors' and all legal rules can be traced back to the determinate individual or group holding absolute power in civil society; sovereign power is unlimited, as 'supreme power limited by positive law, is a flat contradiction in terms'. Law's jurisprudence for Austin is analytical, centred on the descriptive and unexplicated notions of legal right, legal duty and legal validity, which are considered independently of history, politics, social circumstances, morality or metaphysics. There is no attempt to contextualise legal inquiry into the nature of law or its function in social and political life. Law is, therefore, a matter of positive law, and positive law means simply (a) the 'command of the sovereign' having the authority to issue orders, which is (b) backed by the threat of sanction for disobedience.

KEY THEORIST

Hans Kelsen (1881–1973)

Hans Kelsen's normative legal positivism, articulated in his 1934 *Pure Theory of Law*, is recognised as a major legal theory, in which he sought to liberate his 'science of law' from any political, historical or sociological ideology. This is not because he disregarded these influential contexts as irrelevant; rather he sought to avoid the obfuscatory influence of an uncritical assortment of methodologically diverse disciplines of law. To this end, Kelsen proposed a *pure theory of law*, with the emphasis on a 'system of norms' that is not dependent on, for example, moral standards; rather, their normative validity is based on being created in a particular manner and their relationship with other (higher) legal norms. These 'binding norms' exist in a hierarchy of (higher and lower) norms, which indicate how individuals *ought* to behave in all circumstances, and apply to everyone.

Kelsen uses the term 'norm', according to the prescriptive sense of an imperative as that which *ought* to be done, and the content of a norm is not subject to evaluation by any external criteria. His theory equates the existence of law to its validity conditioned by a hierarchy of legal norms, at the top of which is a foundational legal principle, namely the universal *Grundnorm* (in German) or 'basic norm'. The Grundnorm is presupposed by the jurist, and serves as a hypothetical measure or standard for all other 'lower' norms in any legal system, including legal structures, statements, cultures and endeavours. These lower norms, starting with constitutional law, are understood to derive their authority or 'bindingness' from the Grundnorm. So an important question, for Kelsen, concerns not only the validity of a norm, but also its relationship to other norms in the 'system of norms'.

KEY THEORIST

H.L.A. Hart (1907–1992)

Hart's legal theory is sometimes referred to as a neo-positivist theory of law, since his 1960s ground-breaking version of (modern) legal positivism updates that of Austin, which is commonly credited as the starting point for most enquiries into the nature of law. Hart, like Austin, sought to distinguish the descriptive question of what law is from the prescriptive question of what law ought to be; however, he upheld the idea of a normative dimension that is evidenced by a common feeling of obligation to follow the law. That law is a *complex social fact* has immense normative significance for Hart and this idea is central to understanding his articulation and defence of core positivist doctrines; it turns on two aspects relating to (a) the nature of law and (b) the everyday functionality of law.

Hart's thesis determines law as an institutionalised system of rules, which unites 'primary' and 'secondary' rules. Primary rules, generally speaking, require or forbid certain types of behaviour and can motivate duties or obligations. Secondary rules might be described as 'rules about the rules', which allow primary rules to be modified or specify additional criteria appropriate to the wider application of primary rules; these conform to Hart's *rule of recognition* doctrine, as the highest criterion of secondary rules, which facilitates the identification of a valid law. Validity determines which rules should be regarded as laws and, therefore, engenders a critical internal attitude in the citizenry that prompts the assumption of an obligation. In the context of competing primary rules (statute, judicial precedent and constitutional provisions), the rule of recognition plays a significant role in classifying the sources of law and providing a mechanism for distinguishing valid from invalid laws, without taking into account subjective moral grounds. However, whilst a law remains valid even if nobody abides by it, the rule of recognition depends on the acquiescence of, for example, the judiciary, legislature and citizenry, and requires their actions to correspond with its existence and their acceptance of its status as a rule.

KEY DEFINITION: Hart's 'core' and 'penumbra'

For Hart, legal rules are not always certain; they possess both a core and a penumbra. This means all legal rules are established according to words that express a core meaning, and in penumbral cases there is some uncertainty as to the precise meaning of the words. They may be perceived by the interpreter as ambiguous or vague. Hart claims this is always a linguistic issue rather than indicative of any internal contradiction or inconsistency. He asserts that such indeterminacies can be easily resolved by revisiting the words comprising the settled core of meaning, which restricts the possibility of endless disagreements over the meaning of a word.

Hart offered a further explanation that 'the rule of recognition may incorporate, as criteria of legal validity, conformity with moral principles or substantive values in some systems of law … as in the United States, the ultimate criteria of legal validity might explicitly incorporate besides pedigree, principles of justice or substantive moral values, and these may form the content of legal constitutional restraints'. Sex discrimination, for example, is prohibited and backed by legal sanction because it is judged to be immoral, and ordinary moral terms such as 'right' and 'equality' are used to support this view. This means that, for Hart, there is no possibility of law unless some legal officials take a pre-committed point of view, particularly with regard to those legal statements that describe the criteria by which judges are to determine the sources of legal content.

Within Hart's legal theory the jurisprudential undertaking is strictly descriptive, although the law comprises a systemic unity of institutionalised rules that are grounded in social convention and practices and, whilst not morally binding, these exert influence on participators and direct social interaction. Furthermore, it is not necessary to stand entirely inside or outside the law, as it is possible to acknowledge the internal perspective held by others without completely embracing it personally, thereby allowing room for critical distance. This is why Hart's theory is often referred to as 'soft' positivism, since it acknowledges that a rule of recognition may contain moral criteria, and so recognises the influence of morality on legal content.

KEY DEFINITION: Hart's separability thesis

In his 1957 article, *Positivism and the Separation of Law and Morals*, Hart states, 'there is no necessary connection between law and morals or law as it is and ought to be'. This is not the same as saying that law and morals are automatically separate, nor is he arguing for a strict separation between law and morals. After all, as Raz pointed out in his 1979 *The Authority of Law*, 'the claim that what is law ... is purely a matter of social fact still leaves it an open question whether or not those social facts by which we identify the law ... do or do not endow it with moral merit. If they do, [the law] has of necessity amoral character.' Hart's thesis is, therefore, simply promoting moral neutrality, in that general jurisprudence must not be committed in advance to conclusions about the moral value of law. The mission of legal positivism is to advocate truth and clarity in the law which, for Hart, is a 'sovereign virtue in jurisprudence'. As always with jurisprudence, there are many differing views on the separability thesis, which is accused by Hart's critics of being 'hopelessly ambiguous'.

KEY THEORIST

Joseph Raz (b. 1939)

Joseph Raz, in common with Hart, finds that social facts alone determine the identity and content of law. However, his '*sources thesis*' marks a return to 'hard' positivism, evidenced by its claim that 'a jurisprudential theory is acceptable only if its tests for identifying the content of the law and determining its existence depend *exclusively* on the facts of human behaviour capable of being described in value–neutral terms and applied without resort to moral argument'.

The content of an authoritative directive, for Raz, must be identifiable without contemplating the dependent reasons that justify the directive. It excludes not only moral content but the possibility of any evaluative considerations that may influence or justify the identification or determination of a legal rule; even when what is being described is evaluative or normative, moral considerations are extraneous.

For Raz, law is a legitimate authoritative institution; its authority is identifiable on its own terms and legal science is not committed to regarding the law as just. He distinguishes between '*detached*' (external) and '*committed*' (internal) legal statements. Those who accept a legal obligation or duty, without sharing the opinion that underpins it (which may be grounded in the normative language of rights and duties, etc.), are described as having a 'detached point of view' (referred to by Neil MacCormick as the hermeneutic view), against those who accept the rationale in the relevant rule, who are referred to as 'committed'. Adoption of the detached point of view means that, according to Raz, a judge can rule on a sex discrimination case without believing in the immorality of sex discrimination; the application of such concepts as equality and fairness are simply properties of the legal lexicon developed from the law's point of view. Even so, Raz admits that judges, for example, must at least make 'moral claims' on behalf of law when they act in their official capacities. In his 2004 journal article 'Incorporation of law' in *Legal Theory*, he qualifies this assertion, stating that judges need a moral reason to hold themselves answerable to law, but they need no legal reason to hold themselves answerable to moral considerations.

KEY THEORIST

Ronald Dworkin (1931–2013)

Ronald Dworkin was arguably one of the most influential legal theorists of his generation, famous primarily for his sustained anti-positivist stance. He advocated a constructivist theory of jurisprudence that has been characterised as a 'third theory' or middle way between natural law theory and legal positivism. Dworkin's theory centres on criticisms of the positivist elements of H.L.A. Hart's theory of law, such as the 'model of rules', which ignores the value of moral principles that have weight yet are not traceable to any formal authority. Similarly, in adjudicating hard cases, Hart believed discretion belonged with the judiciary, giving them a quasi-legislative function; whereas Dworkin insists that even in hard cases, the law always provides the 'right answer' – as one of the parties has a right to win.

For Dworkin, rights (which he refers to as 'trumps') are more fundamental than rules; and in any conflict, a rights claim should prevail over rules. In his 1977 *Taking Rights Seriously*, he refers to an ideal judge, the metaphorical 'Judge Hercules', who has the ability to decide any case by simply constructing the theory that best fits and justifies the law as a whole (law as integrity). In his later work *Justice for Hedgehogs* (2011), he connects his 'right answer' thesis to moral realism – in other words, the view that moral propositions have actual truth value, which further legitimates their centrality in adjudication.

■ The *Hart* v *Dworkin* debate: a critique of legal positivism

The question at the centre of this significant debate is, 'Is the law ultimately grounded in social facts alone, or do moral facts also determine the existence and content of the law?'. Ronald Dworkin presents his critique of legal positivism in two parts: the first claims that judges often refer to moral principles in deciding legal cases since they feel legally obliged to do so, and the second part alleges that they often disagree as to which moral principles should take precedence in forming the basis for judgment. Whereas Hart regards the law as a social institution based on convention, cohesion and consensus, Dworkin places disagreements centre stage. This does not mean that *all* grounds of law provide an area of conflict, as both Dworkin and legal positivists accept the sanctity of statute, judicial decisions and the legitimate sources of law. This suggestion refers to the 'theoretical disagreements' over the test criteria used for determining the validity of legal norms. Even so, the idea of legal representatives and members of the judiciary at constant loggerheads is a complete anathema to positivists and so Dworkin's claim, made in his 1998 *Law's Empire*, has been the subject of much debate.

Be critical

You can begin to critique Dworkin's view by showing how he confuses too many types of disagreement, which should be dealt with separately for reasons of clarity. You might point out that the basic question of continuing significance remains the same: namely, is law grounded in social facts alone or does a range of more complex moral considerations also determine the existence and content of the law?

Dworkin's chief target is the group of legal positivists he refers to as 'orthodox positivists': those who adhere to the sovereign theory that determines legal validity as fixed by legal officials, who are always in general agreement. Suggesting this state of constant consensus is impossible, Dworkin submits an alternative theory that treats law as an 'interpretive' concept, so that the only correct way to understand law is through the idea of interpretation. Legal officials may argue about the proper meaning attributed to the sources of law (these may include implied or implicit norms such as privileged moral principles that have already been accepted into law in their canonical form), about which interpretation best matches and justifies the legal materials. These are arguments concerning the criteria of legal validity or, in other words, the content of what Hart refers to as the 'rule of recognition'.

Legal positivists counter Dworkin's criticisms by stating that legal disagreements are uncommon and, moreover, a disagreement over the content of the normative provisions of a system first requires an agreement concerning the fact that the system is made up of these provisions. Yet, aside from this abstractly formulated 'master rule' under which there is a general agreement about what counts as a valid legal source, our supreme and constitutional courts are often divided into ideologically divergent parties, each holding divergent views about their interpretation. According to Dworkin, the possibility of theoretical disagreement, so abhorred by legal positivists, renders 'law as integrity' and means our judges are bound to debate the correct interpretation of the law in such a way that it, ideally, reflects a single, coherent set of principles of justice and fairness.

Be critical

A key criticism of Hart is that he neglects the impact of interpretative sentences that offer scope for disagreement. A sentence such as 'no vehicles in the park' implies the possibility of exceptions such as emergency service vehicles and roller skates, or, by analogy, may relate to forms of conveyance such as horses and wheelchairs. It is not always possible, or desirable, to ascribe a single settled meaning to a rule formulation; different sets of values that underpin the rule formulation may give rise to a range of diverse questions, and disagreements, concerning the scope of the meaning of a text or legal statement. You could offer examples: for instance, a seemingly unambiguous term such as 'water' is recognisable in various forms (as lakes, oceans, puddles and on tap), yet if we want to understand its internal structure we must consult other disciplines such as chemistry or literature, where it often has an important metaphoric role, and even to law with its beloved 'floodgates' metaphor.

KEY DEFINITION: The semantic sting

As Hart claims, the normative force of law depends on a shared recognition (by both law-makers and judges) of the appropriate content and validity of legal rules. This presupposes that tests for 'law's truth' are uncontroversial as all lawyers hold exactly the same understanding of the meaning of key words and expressions and, therefore, the grounds of law. So then, for Hart, the language of the law can be meaningful only if lawyers share the same criteria for determining the truth of statements of law.

Alternatively, according to Dworkin, this represents a rather simplistic view of the relationship between law and language because even the word 'law' is an interpretative concept and depends on certain specific criteria. His **semantic sting** argument claims that Hart's concept cannot explain what makes a statement of law true or false, and assumes any real disagreement about the law is impossible. Rather, Dworkin argues that whilst legal discourse attaches to objects and subjects having real properties that can be agreed upon (for example, house, tenant, water), yet there is room for disagreement, by legal theorists and lawyers, as to which concepts may attach to those properties.

Make your answer stand out

It is important to show that you understand how questions that arise within jurisprudence overlap with a range of other disciplines, such as politics, history, literature, philosophy, anthropology and economics. To prepare a good answer, it is necessary to consult original sources that illustrate the richness and diversity of, in this case, legal positivist schools of thought. Only then can you experience first-hand how legal theorists present and argue their views on important notions such as powers, rights, duties and morality. Reading original materials will also further develop your language and reasoning skills.

Be critical

It is important to note that although legal positivists deny the necessity for morality to inform law-making, this does not mean they are unconcerned with moral questions or negate their influence. It simply means they believe the best approach to analysing and understanding the law is to suspend moral judgement, which they find too indeterminate and capricious. So make sure you take into account the limits of legal positivism, those grey areas where legal positivists have admitted the possibility of moral considerations, and be sure to understand their reasoning on this important and contentious issue of separability. Then you will be able to construct your own argumentative position as to why you agree or disagree with a particular interpretation.

□ REVISION NOTE

When consulting original sources for inspiration, read the preface or foreword first in order to ascertain what assumptions are made with regard to the scope and relevance of key themes and how they may add to the existing knowledge on this particular area of jurisprudence. The introductory material usually summarises some basic concepts, which may be helpful in providing an initial condensed overview of complex ideas.

■ Putting it all together

Answer guidelines

See the sample question at the start of the chapter.

Approaching the question

The question is asking you to explain on what grounds legal positivists claim that law is distinct from morality, and the extent to which these justifications differ between early and modern legal philosophers. Added to the comparative aspect is the wider question relating to the desirability and feasibility, or possibility, of moral separatism. The desirability aspect of the essay question refers to the claims of hard positivists and their concerns in relation to validity, certainty and sovereign authority in the identification and formation of legal rules. With reference to feasibility, this is a particularly pertinent question in light of the fact that popular opinion on controversial issues (such as adoption by same-sex couples) is loaded with moral content. More importantly, legal systems claim moral authority for themselves and legal rhetoric is arguably loaded with moral terms. In addition, as soft positivist Hart indicated in *The Concept of Law*, although legal positivists assert that 'it is in no sense a necessary truth that laws reproduce or satisfy certain demands of morality, in fact they have often done so'. Explaining and contrasting the strengths and weaknesses of such claims, according to the differing perspectives afforded by diverse versions of legal positivism, would be at the core of your analytical approach to the question.

Important points to include

Make sure you are familiar with and include:

- ■ Legal positivism as a purely normative inquiry
- ■ The origins and critique of the idea of law as a simple matter of facts and social conventions
- ■ The origins and modern configuration of the classical command theory formulation, relating to either sovereign authority or state-centric hierarchies of power
- ■ A qualification of the characteristic reductionist techniques relating to the determination of legal validity
- ■ The separability thesis; evaluate the proposition that there is no necessary connection between law and morals
- ■ Contrasting the views of key classical and modern legal positivists in relation to the merits and demerits of moral neutrality.

▶

Make your answer stand out

Having described the main facets of legal positivism, you could then offer a critical perspective by emphasising the reductionist project at the heart of legal positivism. This can be traced from Austin's command theory of law, which purports to provide a reduction of law to facts of a social nature, to Hart's theory as a more recent attempt to clarify what law is in terms of observable social behaviour and what constitutes legal processes and institutions. Furthermore, Hart privileges social rules as the foundation of law, which can be explained reductively in terms of the patterns of conduct, beliefs and attitudes of people, and this formula comprises all the necessary ingredients for any legal order. You could then refer to one of Dworkin's main criticisms of legal positivism in *Law's Empire*, which was directed towards Hart's semantic **reductionism**.

Irrespective of whether this was Hart's intention, Dworkin claims Hart ignores the constraints imposed on social explanations by language, and reduces certain statements or idiosyncratic vocabulary, exemplifying a type of (shared) discourse, to a particular privileged and foundational class of discourse. Where discourse functions as authoritative discourse, it ceases to function as information, rules and paradigms, but attempts to determine the foundations of our ideological relations with the world without considering alternative discourses. The corollary of this criticism would be that legal positivism is not open to conceptual analysis on what law is; neither does it entertain the idea of interpretation. Interpretation is commonly linked to the notion of evaluative judgments as to the most persuasive moral justification for a particular legal practice, and the possibility of the multiple significations of key terms that indicate a wider range of unexplicated concepts. The addition of a strong critical perspective based on either an internal or immanent critique, or by reference to one of the movement's key critics such as Dworkin, will offer a more rounded overview of legal positivism and give your answer extra gravitas.

READ TO IMPRESS

Dworkin, R.M. (1986) *Law's Empire*. Cambridge, MA: Harvard University Press, 31–45.

Green, L. (2008) Positivism and the Inseparability of Law and Morals. *New York University Law Review*, 83: 1035–1058.

Hart, H.L.A. (1983) Positivism and the Separation of Law and Morals, in *Essays in Jurisprudence and Philosophy*. Oxford: Oxford University Press, 49–87.

Leiter, B. (2004) Legal Realism, Hard Positivism, and the Limits of Conceptual Analysis, in *Hart's Postscript: Essays on the Postscript to the 'Concept of Law'*. J. Coleman (ed.). Oxford: Oxford University Press, 355–371.

Marmor, A. (2011) Can the Law Imply More Than It Says: On Some Pragmatic Aspects of Strategic Speech, in *Philosophical Foundations of Language in the Law*. A. Marmor and S. Soames (eds). Oxford: Oxford University Press, 83–104.

Patterson, D. (2010) Legal Positivism, in *A Companion to Philosophy of Law and Legal Theory* (Blackwell Companions to Philosophy) 2nd edition. Oxford: Wiley-Blackwell, 228–248.

Postema, G.J. (2012) Legal Positivism: Early Foundations, in *The Routledge Companion to Philosophy of Law*. A. Marmor (ed.). London: Routledge, 31–47.

Shapiro, S.J. (2007) The 'Hart–Dworkin' Debate: A Short Guide for the Perplexed, in *Ronald Dworkin: Contemporary Philosophy in Focus*. A. Ripstein (ed.). Cambridge: Cambridge University Press, 22–55.

Shapiro, S.J. (2011) *Legality*. Cambridge, MA: Harvard University Press, 79–117.

www.pearsoned.co.uk/lawexpress

Go online to access more revision support, including quizzes to test your knowledge, sample questions with answer guidelines, podcasts you can download and more!

Legal realism

Revision checklist

Essential points you should know:

- ☐ Legal realism: discovering the 'truth of law'
- ☐ Law as judge-made
- ☐ American legal realists: Oliver Wendell Holmes and Karl Llewellyn
- ☐ Scandinavian legal realists: Axel Hägerström, Vilhelm Lundstedt and Alf Ross

■ Topic map

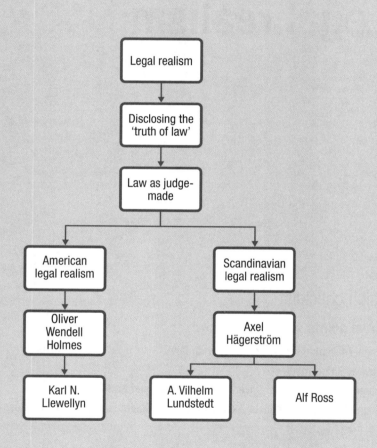

▊ Introduction

Legal realism: telling the 'truth of law' as it really is

Two main schools of thought have emerged as a reaction against the 'lifeless' formalist conception of law as a logical, syllogistic and consistent system of rules and principles. Against this mechanistic and non-political approach to law, *American legal realists* and *Scandinavian legal realists* have both pursued an interest in discovering what the law 'really' is, in terms of the practicalities rather than by appealing to any notion of the right theory. They both attempt to explain law in terms of observable behaviour (analysing cause and effect) and are sceptical about values such as justice and right, as well as being suspicious of metaphysical explanations. The focus is on the actual operation of law in a social context; the significance of common-law adjudication to determining legal and social welfare developments is a main area of concern. Whilst both are sceptical that the legal doctrine invoked by judges in their opinions actually explains their decisions, the American legal realists believe all the interesting developments and hard work take place in the courtroom, where rules and judicial reasoning are pitched against individual cases. As Anthony D'Amato has stated, 'The judge's gavel signifies the brute finality of the court's determination of the law. One does not cavil with a gavel.'

For legal realists, law is indeterminate; legal texts, statutes and precedent do not determine the outcome of legal disputes. Furthermore, since 'the law' does not exist in the physical world – only scientific laws, such as the law of gravity – it is not discoverable in a literal way. There are no readily discernible primordial laws, no pre-existing normative standard to which the facts can be applied towards eliciting a 'predictable' legal supposition. It is perceived as only a social or shared mental construct; in other words, the law is what we, collectively, want it to be; and if we go back one recursive step, we believe that law is what judges believe it to be. In 1897 Oliver Wendell Holmes urged legal scholars to discover the 'truth of law'. The way to achieve this, for legal realists, is to examine 'law in action' rather than rely on 'law in books' (as *res, non verba* or 'actions speak louder than words'). In the spirit of 'law is as law does', the tradition of legal realism seeks to locate law within the social world of 'social reality'. This means judicial decisions are seen as organised around social situations rather than grounded on legal rules and concepts.

Although law is said to be the product of the opinions of judicial decision makers, as well as social, economic and contextual influences – as is the case with other schools of thought within jurisprudence – there are many differences in the interests, fields of work and viewpoints of various legal realists. Also, legal realism is commonly referred to as the precursor to the critical legal studies (CLS) movement, as both are ▶

'rule-sceptics' and challenge law's alleged impartiality. However, many CLS members are more inclined to view politics or ideology as the empirically dominant motivator of judicial decisions, whereas legal realists are persuaded by the influence of psychology (of the judiciary) or social policy factors.

ASSESSMENT ADVICE

An essay or exam question will assume that you understand how legal realism relates to both legal positivism and natural law theory. You need to be able to demonstrate how legal realists, such as Holmes, tend to be suspicious of metaphysics or 'transcendental nonsense', and any reliance upon value-laden considerations in adjudication. Make use of quotations from original sources to support your answer. There is antipathy towards natural law principles and the natural rights traditions, which assume an integral moral relationship with law and the law-making process. Illustrate how, for legal realists, adjudication is only interested in practical outcomes, and moral considerations are little more than 'a state of mind'. Although legal positivism and legal realism are often assumed to be opposite positions, this is based on an assumption that positivists are also formalists, which is not necessarily the case. Explain how both legal realists and positivists share a mutual disdain for the idea of an *essential* connection between law and morals, and both believe law to be a matter of social fact.

■ Sample question

Could you answer this question? Below is a typical essay question that could arise on this topic. Guidelines on answering the question are included at the end of this chapter. Another sample question and guidance on tackling it can be found on the companion website.

ESSAY QUESTION

Discuss the main differences between American and Scandinavian legal realism, and explain how legal realism is distinguished from other influential schools of thought within jurisprudence.

▉ Law is *made* by judges

Legal realists claim that judges *make* law at more frequent intervals than is commonly assumed. There is no eternal pre-existing law upon which all judges, through time, have been able to rely. Although the principle of *stare decisis* (the doctrine of binding precedent) requires judges to follow the ruling of the first court, it still allows them to distinguish their case by introducing a new dimension, or they may take into account other factors. These factors may include a particular idiosyncratic preference – for example, how a particular judge thinks about a certain type of behaviour, their mood, feelings, alliances and whether they are over-precautious or under-precautious. Where a legal rule is established, this has come about as a result of a discretionary judgment that has been conceded by the majority. Consequently, *stare decisis* is viewed by legal realists as a flexible process rather than a hard and fast rule: a judge may incrementally move the rule established in precedents towards his or her own predilections. In this way, case law developments are founded not in binary logic (what is right and wrong), which fixes judicial limits, but rather in rhetorical stratagems that reveal the judges' preferences and influence their incentives.

A change in the law often reflects the implementation of the preferences of the judiciary. An example of this would be the refusal of the English judiciary to implement the provisions of the 1961 Suicide Act in order to penalise persons accompanying a terminally ill spouse/partner/family member to an overseas clinic such as 'Dignitas' (a Swiss euthanasia clinic), contrary to the provisions of s.2(1) – '*A person who aids, abets, counsels or procures the suicide of another, or attempt by another to commit suicide shall be liable on conviction on indictment to imprisonment for a term not exceeding fourteen years*'. Although the House of Lords was unable to agree on an amendment or repeal of the 1961 Act, the Director of Public Prosecutions was forced to issue sentencing guidelines in 2010, following the landmark case of *R (on application of Purdy)* v *Director of Public Prosecutions* [2010] 1 AC 345. The guidelines are based on a set of public interest factors, which formally acknowledge the judges' preference to not apply s.2(1).

For legal realists, to understand the law it is necessary to observe judicial behaviour and examine the patterns of decisions revealed in actual cases as these are the most reliable guides to, and the most accurate basis for, predicting how future courts will behave.

▉ American legal realism

American legal realism was one of the most important intellectual movements of the twentieth century. It emerged in the United States in the 1920s and 1930s and challenged ideas about legal reasoning and adjudication that were dominant in legal practice and academic writing at that time. It comprises a collection of theories that present the nature of law and legal reasoning as, largely, indeterminate.

Brian Leiter distinguishes two types of indeterminacy. The first relates to *rational* indeterminacy, in the sense that the available class of legal reasons did not *justify* a unique decision; and the second proposes the law to be also *causally* or explanatorily indeterminate, in that legal reasons were not sufficient to explain why judges decided as they did. This does not mean a legal system is completely unpredictable, rather it means that one needs to know what to look at in order to predict the law – even if legal categories are simply 'empty vessels' containing 'acts of power that force meaning into them', as long as 'power' can be analysed, then the law can be predicted in some way. However, this depends on what can be identified as a 'legal source'; in addition, taking into account that judges are more likely to respond primarily to the stimulus of the facts of the case as opposed to strict legal rules and reasons. Legal realists were (generally) clear that their focus was placed on **law's indeterminacy** (see page 92) at the stage of appellate review, where a degree of uncertainty in the law was more likely.

The protagonists were social scientists and lawyers who were countering the dominant formalistic approach to law-making, which did not allow for the judges reaching a decision based on, for example, their own assumptions as to what was 'fair' in relation to the fact of the case. Unlike the Scandinavians, who were philosophers, the American legal realists never made explicit philosophical presuppositions concerning the nature of law or attempted to explicate a conception of legal theory. Emphasis is placed on the specific facts of cases and conventions of social institutions, in order to discover what *really* motivates judicial decision-making. Many thought legal science should emulate the *empirical testing* methods of the natural sciences in being able to test any hypothesis against an observation of the world.

American jurist and associate justice of the US Supreme Court, Oliver Wendell Holmes, is commonly considered to be the most important forerunner of American legal realism; other significant legal realists include Karl Llewellyn, Benjamin Cardozo, Jerome Frank, Felix Cohen, Herman Oliphant and Roscoe Pound. The latter's famous dictum related to 'real' judicial decision-making processes as 'law in action', which had nothing in common with 'law in books'.

KEY DEFINITION: Formalism

There are various degrees and types of **formalism**: however, in general, legal formalists believe law to be autonomous, comprehensive, logically ordered and determinate – law is treated as a lifeless phenomenon. Legal formalists express the view that judges and other public institutions should confine their deliberations to interpreting legal texts, such as statute and case law, which describe what the law *is*. Judges must only engage in pure mechanical deduction from this body of law to produce single correct conclusions. They should constrain any tendency towards activism, only seeking to find and apply the appropriate legal rule and refrain from interpreting what they believe the law *ought* to be. The only interpretative context, by which meaning can be attributed to an abstract concept, is that which existed at the time of a rule's inception. Therefore, the domain of interpreting law is separated from the policy considerations that formed the law, and is characterised by strict adherence to the law of precedent and procedural propriety.

KEY THEORIST

Oliver Wendell Holmes, Jr (1841–1935)

Holmes opposed the view of law as a broad abstract concept, and attacked the proposition that all legal provisions could be rationally defended according to some conceptually deductive process – claiming there are no objective standards that can determine right and wrong, so the idea of 'just' answers to legal questions is misleading. He advocated a form of moral **scepticism**, which stands in sharp contrast to theories of natural law; asserting moral concerns have nothing to do with law as they amount to little more than a state of mind. The only way to understand legal duty and legal right is to keep them completely separate from the corresponding moral concepts; this idea has obvious synergies with legal positivism. Holmes famously declared, in his influential 1881 work *The Common Law*, that 'the life of the law has not been logic, it has been experience' and repudiated the notion of the common law as a 'brooding omnipresence in the sky', insisting that the focus of law should be as it is practised.

In supporting his view that legal matters should be kept completely separate from any conception of values (morals) or **metaphysics** (see page 90), Holmes recommended in his seminal *The Path of the Law* that the law be viewed as if through the eyes of a 'bad man' who cares only 'for the material consequences which such knowledge enables him to predict' – in other words, what the courts are 'likely to do in fact'. He further warned against viewing law as a good man 'who finds his reasons for conduct, whether inside the law or outside of it, in the vaguer sanctions of conscience'. The fact-oriented and context-specific nature of judicial decision-making was, therefore, the main thrust of his realism. However, although he separated law and morality, Holmes did not view the internal (fact) and external (moral) approaches to law as mutually exclusive. He understood the legal reality of courts having to formulate policies that must balance the conflicting interests of different classes and ideologies in society – which was better achieved by judges being motived by their *experience* of the comparative worth and importance of competing legislative grounds for meeting social needs and values.

Accordingly, Holmes believed that since the personal and political preferences of members of the judiciary were, either consciously or subconsciously, instrumental in determining legal outcomes, then the social sciences and public policy should have a larger role. This was a critique of legal reasoning, in that legal rules were too often indeterminate and judges had to rely on other more personal sources such as a hunch or bias. Furthermore, since judges make a decision based on what they believe to be the correct answer *after* hearing a case, only then do they find appropriate law to lend support to their decision. In this way the law does not exist in the present, it only comes into existence in the future – this means that in the present, we have to make *prophecies* as to how we believe the law might turn out. The predictive nature of law was the thesis of Holmes' acclaimed 1897 article, *The Path of the Law*, which confirmed that the object of the study of law is 'prediction, the prediction of the incidence of the public force [reward or punishment] through the instrumentality of the courts'.

Make your answer stand out

Holmes was a major figure in a sceptical revolution that greatly influenced American jurisprudence. His writings have produced much memorable prose. For example, supporting his view of law as simply pricing he stated 'taxes are the price we pay for civilised society', and in *The Path of the Law* Holmes claimed that we should look at law from the perspective of a self-interested bad man who cares only about material consequences. It is possible to find various online journal articles by academics who have sought to 'find the good' in Holmes' 'bad man', indicating a range of interpretative approaches to his thesis. You will also make your answer stand out by quoting some of his famous expressions to support your answer.

KEY THEORIST

Karl Llewellyn (1893–1962)

Karl Llewellyn was a mainstream realist who believed that law should reflect the *'reality'* of society; he referred to legal rules (apart from serving as predictions of what the judges may decide) as merely 'pretty playthings'. Like Holmes, he rejected the 'blind imitation of the past' that served to limit 'the possibilities of our imagination'. As an admirer of the common law tradition, he sought to emulate the Aristotelian practical-wisdom decision-making model on which the common law is based. His functionalist account elucidates law as an 'organised activity' undertaken by greater and lesser legal actors for a variety of legal purposes.

In his 1960 book *The Common Law Tradition: Deciding Appeals*, Llewellyn identifies two pillars that evince two distinct styles of deciding cases, according to the role performed by the relevant legal actor. One pillar concerns the 'grand style' of adjudication, whereby judges are inculcated with the content of law, and immersed in the culture to the extent that modes of argumentation are internalised. These exert a profound influence so that lawyers in the same system (for example, in the appellate court) will act in a similar way to each other when deciding similar cases. The judges engage with policy considerations, often on matters of constitutional importance, so the very existence of society depends on this level of institutional law-making. The other pillar concerns what Llewellyn refers to as *crafts*; these are minor institutions that are characterised by their specialist nature and treatment of legal rules as formal and prescriptive. Together they make up part of a distinct cultural system for assigning meaning to events that take place in the daily lives of individuals.

Llewellyn was preoccupied with law as a 'technology' rather than a 'philosophy' and so insisted that law is an engine that has 'purposes' and 'not values in itself'. In support of this view, he asserted that law functioned as a major social institution that not only had responsibilities for ensuring the preservation of the legal community, but also assumed a wider societal obligation. He referred to the basic functions of law as 'law jobs', with the aim of using this relatively simple theoretical framework to analyse and assess the legal institution's contribution to, and achievements within, society – relating to, for example, justice, efficacy and the greater good of all members of society. As a curious mixture of vagueness and specificity, critics have said that this model of law overlooks the structures of dimension and power in society. However, Llewellyn's attempt to articulate the processes of adjudication, appropriateness of law-making, application of rules and, *inter alia*, the function of law in social development and welfare at the local level – if not perfect – has been commended in its embracing of law's structural pluralism, which contains the possibility of limiting the coercive effects of law.

KEY DEFINITION: Karl Llewellyn's 'law jobs'

A wide range of **'law jobs'** examples are found in Llewellyn's 1941 *The Normative, The Legal and The Law Jobs: The Problem of Juristic Method*; however, many authors tend to refer to just some of the main examples. Llewellyn regards such law jobs as implicit in the concept of any group activity and takes his inspiration from contemporary social science. Below are some of those basic functions the law has to perform.

- Prevent and avoid 'trouble cases', such as destabilising conflicts, by channelling conduct and expectations within the community. This may relate to practical measures, such as traffic regulations to facilitate effective public transportation.

- Resolve disputes when these arise between members of the community. The rules governing contract are a good example of ways in which the judicial machinery is able to limit the power of business in the marketplace, to ensure individual freedom in bargaining and protection for the weaker party.

- The organisation of society to provide the possibility of integration, direction and incentive – for example, by enacting legislation that prohibits racial discrimination on one hand and by the establishment of social welfare systems on the other. Such legal frameworks stimulate human interaction for the benefit of the individual and society.

- The allocation of authority and establishment of specific procedures that are recognised and accepted within the community; it is important that, under certain circumstances, law has the 'authoritative say'.

- Establish procedural rules (a juristic method) for performing other tasks within the legal organisation such as those of judge, counsellor, legislator or advocate, who all have different ideas of legal rules and how these should be performed.

Be critical

Llewellyn's theory of legal realism is very important; however, you can critique the major premises on the basis that they are, curiously, too vague *and* too specific. This means that a lawyer would struggle to argue a case effectively because of the need to address every possible factor that may affect the outcome.

■ Scandinavian legal realism

The Scandinavians laid great emphasis on articulating their opposition to metaphysical idealists who believed the nature of reality depended on the human mind and its categories. Their main interest was in traditional philosophical questions about the nature of law and how to locate it within a naturalistic worldview, one that is more or less as described by the physical sciences – in other words, to determine law as a legal science, based only on observable fact and events in the realm of causality.

Unlike the American legal realists who were interested in discovering what really happens when the courts decided cases, Scandinavian legal realists were more interested in the theoretical operation of the legal system as a whole and were hostile to all modes of conceptual thinking, which they viewed as metaphysical or ideological. This is why they have been referred to as 'armchair theorists' because, although they agree that legal rules do not decide cases, their mode of inquiry does not stray far beyond the speculative world of European philosophy.

KEY DEFINITION: Metaphysics

Metaphysics originates from Greek words, indicating 'beyond' and 'physics' – thus, what comes after appearance, or is outside (beyond) objective experience. There are many specific forms; however, in general, metaphysics is a branch of philosophy that deals with the difficult questions of 'being' and 'the world', and so addresses first principles such as: what is the nature of reality, and how can we know or experience the world? Without being able to interpret or acquire knowledge of the world around us, we would be unable to deal with reality; we would not know how to act or obtain food for ourselves. A metaphysical approach to a legal problem would be to ask how is it possible to *know* the truth of legal content and what makes legal content true?

The Scandinavian school of legal realism emerges from the work of Swedish philosopher and jurist, Axel Hägerström, whose influence could be summarised as 'law is a social phenomenon ultimately relying only on the sanction of man himself'. This view is shared by his followers Vilhelm Lundstedt (1882–1955), Karl Olivecrona (1897–1980), Alf Ross (1899–1979) and Ingemar Hedenius (1908–1982).

Axel Hägerström (1868–1939)

Axel Hägerström rejected metaphysics, stating it is impossible to prove a value judgement, what one ought or ought not to do, as true or false because it does not exist in a particular time or space. He further claimed that all value judgements (especially those relating to 'right' and 'duty') incorporated an emotive element and, whilst adopting the form of judgements, could not stand up to any 'factual' test. For example, a 'right to property' does not mean the government will protect your belongings, only that it will assist you to regain them if lost or stolen. Similarly, if a person owes you money, the state cannot guarantee they will pay on time. The right is only a precondition for the protection; the protection is not a precondition for the right.

Although he repudiated the 'command' or sovereign 'will theories' of the positivist tradition, Hägerström agreed with their idea that law must be approached only as a matter of positive fact. Hägerström's ideas were based on Greek and Roman sources of law and he was keen to dismiss the framework of the *jus civile* as a system of rules for obtaining and using supernatural powers. Much of the law was dismissed as an exploitative 'ritualistic exercise', with the notion of a 'legal right' based on nothing more than myth and superstition.

Following in the footsteps of Axel Hägerström, Vilhelm Lundstedt claimed there was no objective way to define the requirements of justice, and that invocations of justice obscured purely subjective preferences or metaphysical claims. Rather, he insisted that law and legislation should be guided by social aims and be directed towards developing a method of social welfare, centred on the objective study of social conditions. This was purported to be the most effective way in which law could, in practical terms, improve society for all its members.

Anders Vilhelm Lundstedt (1882–1955)

Anders Vilhelm Lundstedt viewed rights and duties as merely the outcome of legal rules; as not having an objective existence outside the law and so incapable of being used as justificatory concepts that could determine the content of the law. In his analysis of *Rylands and Fletcher* [1868] LR 3 HL 330 in his 1956 *Legal Thinking Revised*, Lundstedt asserts that all the courts had done is decide what the rule for damages should be in cases relating to escaping danger. The general consensus of the court that their legal reasoning was based on the obligation of the property owner was argued, by Lundstedt, to be 'illusory and superfluous'. Furthermore, it was alleged that the provision of a false legal basis for a decision made otherwise (an after-the-fact rationalisation) only serves to mystify the law and obscure the nature of its power – an approach that was said to be harmful.

Alf Ross (1899–1979)

In common with other Scandinavian realists, Ross offers a systematically misshapen image of the nature of law; however, it comprises a more readily acceptable theory of law. Two distinctive branches of knowledge are proposed in his 1958 *On Law and Justice*. One relates to jurisprudence in a narrow sense (law in a textbook where the law is stated), in other words, the law of norms that merely describe what the law ought to be – so these normative propositions are *about* law. The other concerns itself with law in action and only this legal knowledge is prescriptive as it is *of* law – law that is actually in force, such as a rule contained in a statute. For Ross, unlike his fellow realists, the 'two viewpoints mutually presuppose each other'. Although the doctrinal study of law is interested in ideology, he accepts that the latter is always 'an abstraction from social reality' and so can be useful in helping to 'discover invariant correlations in the law in action'.

Adding to the earlier work of Hägerström and Lundstedt, Ross claimed that legal rules are rules that concern the exercise of force and as such are not addressed to private individuals but only to legal officials; their adherence is based on 'the experience of validity'. For example, a statutory prohibition against theft is implied in the rule that directs the courts or other legal agencies in how to deal, in the requisite manner, with any case of theft brought before them. They must simply observe independent 'directives' that relate to 'norms of competence' and 'norms of conduct'; there is no attempt to fashion a first principle or primary rule relating to theft. The two components of such a directive are the idea of an action (the theft) and an imperative symbol (ought, duty, offence), which are treated as merely words on paper. Such 'schemes of interpretation' enable ordinary people to predict the behaviour of legal actors, such as judges. The only 'reality' to which law corresponds is a psychological reality; that which is connected to the psychological response of the individual who experiences sensations of compulsion or restraint when considering the idea of acting in relation to a given legal provision.

The idea of the *logical* indeterminacy of law refers to the belief that legal rules are so indeterminate that they fail to impose any meaningful constraint on judicial decision-making. In other words, there is no uniquely right answer for any legal problem until determined by statute or legal judgment. This 'after-the-fact rationalisation' (according to hastily provided legal justification for a decision already made by other means, e.g., idiosyncratic bias, preference or intuition) obscures or mystifies the 'real' reason for the decision of the court. This may have significant implications for highly emotive and controversial issues such as abortion or capital punishment.

It does not follow, however, that realists believe all cases are decided in this way; judges will often apply existing legal rules and principles to situations that seem to be familiar (for example, less contentious matters) without much thought or consideration. As Llewellyn states, difficulty arises when the 'cases do not line up this clearly and semi-automatically', then they 'call for intellectual labour'. This is why legal realists aim their critique of law mainly at the level of the appellate court and towards the application of constitutional rules, where complex discussions on novel or divisive issues mostly take place.

 Make your answer stand out

Identify the key realist claims and subject them to critical analysis – for example the predictive nature of law. Show, by reference to leading academic sources, original sources and/or case law examples, how legal reasoning may be viewed as operating in reverse; from intuition or bias of the judges based on the facts of a case, towards a rationalisation of the decision with a hastily found supporting legal rule. Contrast evidence that supports this view of adjudication (which believes law to have only the appearance of 'logic') with the arguments of critics who believe this is a fundamental misunderstanding of the court's interpretative function and wider contribution to legal theory.

Be critical

H.L.A. Hart has criticised the American legal realists, dismissing their rule scepticism as unsound. He asserts that their claims relating to the mythical nature of law and its predictive (uncertain and arbitrary) character are misrepresentations and not grounded on proper empirical research. Brian Leiter (see reference sources in 'Read to impress') has provided a constructive reinterpretation of the main claims that support American legal realism, which provides an answer to such criticisms.

■ Putting it all together

Answer guidelines

See the sample question at the start of the chapter.

Approaching the question

You may begin by describing what distinguishes legal realism from other legal theories, namely the emphasis on the 'real'. You can then explain how realists wanted the legal profession to spend more time considering how law appears at ground level, for ordinary people. For example, to the average citizen the law is simply a prediction as to what the court may decide in their case, rather than being the result of theoretical or moral deliberation. You can then discuss how judges must often look for answers beyond legal rules, relying on their own personal feelings and instincts, whilst realists call for a more scientific basis for law. It is also important to address the main differences between realism and natural law, as well as the differences and similarities with legal positivism. It would be pertinent to discuss the claims of those who say the critical legal movement is the 'new' realism and the arguments of those who disagree.

Explain the common areas of agreement between Scandinavian and American realists. Use examples, such as both were hostile to legal formalism and both were keen to explain law by reference to practicalities rather than by reference to theoretical premises. They also agreed that moral considerations, values and metaphysics had no place in law-making, and both sought to explain the law in terms of observable behaviour and the operation of law in a social context, with some interest in the general notion of promoting social welfare. Discuss how legal realism is a broad concept, and points of departure are mainly concerned with methodology and ideology.

You can refer to examples that illustrate how American realists were mainly concerned with adjudication and practical outcomes (how judges reach their decisions), whilst the Scandinavians were particularly interested in analysing fundamental legal concepts, such as the concept of law, a legal rule or a legal right. They also investigated the 'psychological conditioning' potential of law as an idea imprinted on the human mind. Explore the idea that this approach to legal realism reflected their academic and philosophical roots, as opposed to the professional nature (most were members of the judiciary) of the major influences in the American movement – who were more concerned to propose a simple yet radical alternative view of legal interpretation.

Important points to include

Make sure you are familiar with the following general points of contrast, relating to the nature and process of adjudication.

Conventional perspective

- Judges apply only the law that is made by others.
- Decision-making is a passive exercise as judges are bound by pre-existing law.
- Judges can only amend law within the parameters of limited discretion.
- The legislature is the only legal body that can make new law.
- The process of adjudication is mechanical, logical and based on the application of deductive reasoning.
- Judges must apply the law, as made by the legislature, with impartiality.

Realist perspective

- Adjudication is neither logical nor deductive.
- Judges are not impartial; they often act on personal bias and a 'feeling' towards fairness.
- Judicial decision-making is not inhibited by any pre-existing law.
- Judges do not just find the law, they both make and amend it.
- Statutes and legal sources are not law until the courts declare they are law.
- What a statute requires cannot be properly specified until the courts determine the 'correct' interpretation and apply it.

 Make your answer stand out

It would be a good idea to present a historical context relating to the origins of realism, which constitute a reaction against the nineteenth-century obsession with cultivating law as a neat 'symmetrical structure of logical propositions'. Being resolutely anti-doctrinal and anti-conceptual, realists hold that judicial statements of a rule of law conceal, rather than explain, the basis of a legal judgment. Any application to theory is rejected as a gimmick by the American movement and myth-making by the Scandinavians. It is also suggested by his detractors that Holmes was simply a 'rule nihilist' who believed law was nothing other than the power of the state to coerce behaviour – with the judges' imposition of law on litigants viewed, more or less, as an abuse of power. This is one reason offered as to why some legal scholars trace the roots of the critical legal studies movement (CLS) to realism. ▶

Legal realism was seen as a catalyst for change, a rebellion against the arbitrariness of legal judgment at that time, just as the CLS movement can be understood as a return to the primary intellectual insights of realism – connected with the idea that modern law is a collection of beliefs and prejudices that disguises the arbitrariness and mythical status of law and adjudication processes (which too often lead to social injustice) with a mask of legitimacy. There are many interpretations of legal realism and a good range of academic authorities on this topic; be sure to read widely in order to be able to present a good overview of the main themes, which support your own comparative analysis of legal realism, its limits and contemporary relevance.

READ TO IMPRESS

D'Amato, A. (1978) The Limits of Legal Realism. *Yale Law Journal*, 7(3): 468–513.

D'Amato, A. (2009) Legal Realism Explains Nothing. *Washington University Jurisprudence Review*, 1(1): 1–15.

Green, M.S. (2005) Legal Realism as a Theory of Law. *William and Mary Law Review*, 46(6): 1915–1939.

Holmes, O.W. (1897) Path of the Law. *Harvard Law Review*, 10: 457–478.

Jimenez, M. (2011) Finding the Good in Holmes's Bad Man. *Fordham Law Review*, 79(5): 2069–2080, 2103–2120.

Leiter, B. (2005) American Legal Realism, in *The Blackwell Guide to the Philosophy of Law and Legal Theory*. M.P. Golding and W.A. Edmundson (eds). Oxford: Blackwell, 50–61.

Leiter, B. (2007) Rethinking Legal Realism: Toward a Naturalized Jurisprudence, in *Naturalizing Jurisprudence: Essays on American Legal Realism and Naturalism in Legal Philosophy*. Oxford: Oxford University Press, 15–58.

Strang J. (2009) Two Generations of Scandinavian Legal Realists. *Retfærd Årgang*, 32(1): 62–82.

Tamanaha, B.Z. (2009) Understanding Legal Realism. *Texas Law Review*, 87(4): 731–786.

Twining, W. (2012) *Karl Llewellyn and the Realist Movement (Law in Context Series)* 2nd edition. New York: Cambridge University Press, 3–9, 375–387.

www.pearsoned.co.uk/lawexpress

Go online to access more revision support, including quizzes to test your knowledge, sample questions with answer guidelines, podcasts you can download and more!

Sociological jurisprudence

7

Revision checklist

Essential points you should know:

- [ ] The origins and nature of the relationship between sociology and law
- [ ] What distinguishes 'living law' or law in (a social) context from law in books
- [ ] The importance of understanding law as a social enterprise
- [ ] Key theorists, such as Pound, Durkheim, Marx, Weber and Luhmann, and their distinguishing characteristics
- [ ] The significance of sociological jurisprudence today and examples of the main contemporary scholars, such as Foucault, Habermas and Bourdieu

Topic map

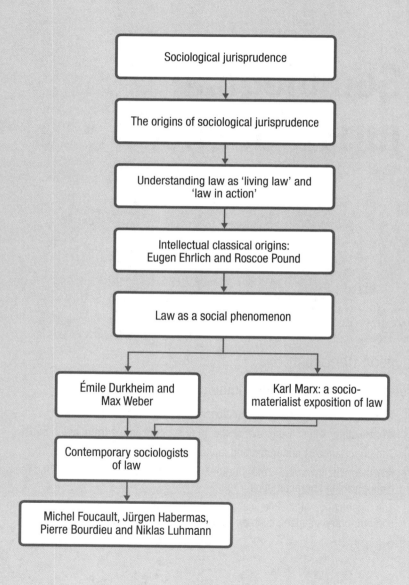

Sociological jurisprudence

The origins of sociological jurisprudence

Understanding law as 'living law' and 'law in action'

Intellectual classical origins: Eugen Ehrlich and Roscoe Pound

Law as a social phenomenon

Émile Durkheim and Max Weber

Karl Marx: a socio-materialist exposition of law

Contemporary sociologists of law

Michel Foucault, Jürgen Habermas, Pierre Bourdieu and Niklas Luhmann

A printable version of this topic map is available from **www.pearsoned.co.uk/lawexpress**

■ Introduction

Sociological jurisprudence: law as 'living law'

The term 'sociological jurisprudence' describes a particular philosophical approach to understanding law as a 'living' concept. In general, supporters of this view believe law to comprise a matrix of relationships found in ordinary everyday life: for example, societies, organisations and interactions between people and institutions. They prioritise the idea of 'law in context' rather than law based on a system of legal norms, more commonly expressed as 'law in books'.

French jurist Friedrich Carl von Savigny held that all positive law, in one sense or another, originates from the *people* and transforms itself in the same manner of language and morals. In the words of modern legal theorist Roger Cotterrell, sociological jurisprudence is 'the systematic, theoretically grounded, empirical study of law as a set of social practices or as an aspect or field of social experience'. This school of thought examines the social effects of legal institutions, doctrines and practices and, conversely, the influence of social phenomena on both substantive and procedural aspects of law-making.

ASSESSMENT ADVICE

The scale and range of literature generated by legal sociologists or sociologists of law is immense. A good answer will demonstrate an understanding of the origins and key sources that make up the landscape of sociological jurisprudence, or the broader law and social theory. You will be able to show an awareness of the main themes explored by a diverse range of theorists, from Roscoe Pound, Émile Durkheim, Max Weber and Niklas Luhmann to Roberto Unger and Jürgen Habermas. Such theorists represent a variety of social science disciplines, for example politics, linguistics, economics as well as sociology, which argue that law is necessarily a social phenomenon rather than a closed and self-referential system of rules and principles.

A common justification for its interdisciplinary nature is that law cannot, legitimately, behave autonomously because of having to interact with other fields of knowledge and social systems. Many theories have critically engaged with others from within the same field, as well as with alternative jurisprudential schools. As is usual with any jurisprudence essay or exam question, for every strong claim it is good practice to refer to the, often equally persuasive, criticisms and counter-claims levelled at a given theoretical position.

◼ Sample question

Could you answer this question? Below is a typical essay question that could arise on this topic. Guidelines on answering the question are included at the end of this chapter, whilst a sample essay question and guidance on tackling it can be found on the companion website.

ESSAY QUESTION

The relationship between law and society is paradoxical because the legal system asserts its autonomy and closure from the extra-legal world, yet as a 'field of knowledge production' it must engage with other fields of knowledge, social institutions, organisations and human behaviour. Discuss how a sociological perspective can enhance our understanding of law.

◼ The origins of sociological jurisprudence

The tradition of considering law as a social institution goes back as far as John Locke, David Hume, even Plato and the Ancient Greeks. Charles-Louis de Secondat, Baron de La Brède et de Montesquieu (commonly referred to only by his last name, Montesquieu) is often considered to be the forerunner of sociological jurisprudence, by representing law as a form of social life properly understood within a physical context, in his radical 1748 treatise, *L'Esprit des Lois*. He sought to explain legal rules, principles and institutions by reference to the social environment in which they operated, and held that in order to 'master legislation' it was first necessary to understand the causes of the existence of law. This leads to two central questions – namely, (a) how law is to be constituted to fit its outward conditions and (b) how it is necessarily shaped by those conditions?

In the US, Roscoe Pound is mooted to be the most influential authority on sociological jurisprudence. Amongst his European counterparts are *inter alia* Hermann Kantorowicz and Eugen Ehrlich, who both challenged the central position of legal formalism by recasting law as a social science, 'people's law' and not a privileged discipline. Ehrlich explained that the 'great mass of law arises immediately in society itself in the form of a spontaneous ordering of social relations, of marriage, the family associations, possession, contracts, succession, and most of this Social Order has never been embraced in Legal Provisions'.

Sociological jurisprudence goes against the self-referential nature of positivist modern law and formalism; a formalistic type of adjudication only serves to isolate judicial reasoning from social needs, interests and consequences. Neither sovereign force nor political decisions determine the content and development of the law; rather, as sociological theorists have pointed out, a range of alternative sociologically grounded disciplinary fields and everyday human behaviour influence adjudication, law-in-practice and the development of jurisprudence. This is viewed as the case even if enforcement is only by habit, social pressure or mutual agreement. By taking an external view, the sociological approach to jurisprudence, the problem of the social is made central to the problem of law's nature. As such, it is useful in enabling us to understand law as 'social law', as a fundamentally social structure determined by social forces that appeals to a diverse range of legitimating rhetoric.

KEY DEFINITION: The sociological perspective

The **sociological perspective** contains three important principles:

1. The way in which society is structured, *social organisation*, comprises a range of institutions: cultural, political, economic and legal.
2. *Social stratification* means these institutions interact with and influence each other on a number of levels. This often produces disagreement, which can result in, for example, forms of discrimination and class conflict.
3. Such institutions and clusters may be analysed in terms of their specific *social function* – for example, the role of state in relation to press freedom v. privacy.

KEY THEORIST

Eugen Ehrlich (1862–1922)

For Ehrlich, sociological jurisprudence means that all social institutions must be given equal weight. Social practice, organisation and context are prioritised as determinants of a lawful society, above coercive force. This means that, unlike Hobbes, he viewed law not as a product of the state or sovereign authority; rather, he defined law as social and the preserve of a society that pre-dates and is logically prior to the state.

Ehrlich provides examples of 'social laws' grounded in the 'living law' (non-state law), which, whilst not always promulgated as statute or precedent (state law), were nevertheless observed and enforced. The law of contract, for example, may be based on 'norms for decision' that are found in statute and case law; however, businessmen rely less on the rules of offer and acceptance, rather on the more informal idea of a 'gentleman's agreement' and good conduct to promote and sustain healthy commercial relationships.

KEY DEFINITION: Ehrlich's 'living law'

For Ehrlich, the living law has enormous influence because it goes beyond the confines of statute and judgment, by regulating all social life and producing social norms or norms of behaviour that govern all social relations. Whereas the courts use legal norms for decision-making in order to resolve disputes only when cases are brought before them, the reality of the living law (as 'law beyond the law') is continually manifested in current social custom.

▶

Our social associations with others (based on family, cultural, religious and political affinities) evidence an 'inner order' that determines a range of rules. What constitutes a 'valid' marriage is determined by people who consider themselves married, in spite of what the law may dictate (for example, same-sex and common-law unions). This wider conception of the law, incorporating contemporary social norms, is considered by Ehrlich to be necessary for maintaining a stable, peaceful and reciprocal society.

KEY THEORIST

Roscoe Pound 1870–1964

American jurist and sociologist Roscoe Pound has much in common with Eugen Ehrlich, whose 'living law' is very similar to the former's 'law-in-action'. Pound criticised the judicial system's disregard of actual facts in favour of rigorous logical deduction, and proposed a new jurisprudence that prioritised the adapting of legal principle and doctrines to the human conditions they are meant to govern, rather than to simply assume first principles. He described the sociological movement in jurisprudence as 'a movement for pragmatism as a philosophy of law' or 'law in action', because it was concerned with 'ends' or the practical social consequences of legal decisions.

Pound developed a 'theory of interests', which legitimises forms of social control such as law, only when founded on informed consideration of relevant competing social interests. Taking into consideration social change and other appropriate social scientific data, as well as the interpretation of precedent and established legal principle, ensures that the law is compatible with this pragmatic ideal – which also fulfils the requirements of a theory of justice.

KEY THEORY

Jural postulates and interests theory

Roscoe Pound's 'jural postulates of a civilised society' are necessary for implementing his theory of interests – a complex scheme that aims to balance public interests (including law and State regulation) and social interests (safety, health and welfare) against individual interests. These jural postulates are not rules; rather, they are ideas of right that reflect society at a given time, and made effective by jurists taking into consideration such factors as the existing social and economic environment. For Pound, rights precede law as legislation. They are grounded in human nature and conduct, and are said to form the basis for all law because they represent a unified legal criteria for balancing conflicting interests, based on a set of contemporary shared needs.

Pound's theory of interests and jural postulates could be described as comprising a 'practical natural law' – albeit with a changing and developing content, unlike the rigidity that characterised mainstream natural law in the eighteenth and nineteenth centuries.

Be critical

You could point out that, although Roscoe Pound's classification is often viewed as useful, there have been various criticisms; for example, there is no consensus in society from which clear sets of interests can be derived and there is little difference between public and social interests. Also, the process of recognising an interest is vague, as an activity may be permitted without being recognised by the law.

■ The difference between sociological jurisprudence and the sociology of law

The *sociology of law* combines two discrete entities. Sociology comprises various fields within the social sciences and aims to gain knowledge about society, how societies are formed and function. Law tends towards the practical; being concerned with legal facts, rule-making and dispute resolution in order to maintain social order – it has little or nothing to say about anything outside itself. Together, as the sociology of law, they address the main debates within the social sciences in order to critically analyse the scope and role of law in society.

Sociological jurisprudence, on the other hand, locates discussion of the social effects on the development of law and legal practice from within the context of law and legal theory, and not social science. Although it includes the construction of hypotheses on which to base the formulation of general laws as they impact on society, it also addresses the practical administrative or legislative issues.

Reza Banakar has suggested these are artificial distinctions in that, although each sociological and broader socio-theoretic approach is distinctive, they share the idea that law functions both as an instrumental and symbolic means of constituting and representing the social order. Both attempt to systematically explicate the nature of law in relation to particular non-legal formulations (social, cultural, political and economic) as part of the social framework.

! Don't be tempted to . . .

There is little uniformity in the use of expressions that describe this idea of law and social theory. Sociology of law, sociological jurisprudence, legal sociology and even socio-legal theory are often used interchangeably. Avoid being distracted by this semantic inconsistency by making sure you understand the general significance of a sociological approach to law, and the various theories that define the relationship between law and the social sciences.

■ What makes law a social phenomenon?

Lawyers tend to refer to concepts that derive from law itself, such as legal rights, duty, property, persons and power. Bearing in mind that the law is committed to providing a minimum standard of justice, for legal sociologists this is only possible by analysing legal structures and concepts against the social conditions within which laws are developed and applied. The social nature and function of law requires examining societal, as well as legal, concepts such as role, group, class and interest. So a comparative study of the ratio of male to female judicial appointments or the take-up of legal aid across different social classes would typically be the subject of socio-legal or legal sociological research. Any general propositions gleaned from such a detailed study would then inform the content of sociological jurisprudence.

KEY THEORIST

Émile Durkheim (1858–1917)

Durkheim believed the evolution of society to be 'spontaneous' and that social bonds can be 'solidified but not created'. He was concerned, therefore, with the idea of what binds society together and understood law as an external index that symbolises the nature of *social solidarity* in any society in which it exists. He identified two forms – namely, 'mechanical solidarity' and 'organic solidarity'. Mechanical solidarity comprises a 'collective consciousness' in which society is organised collectively and members all share the same values as in non-secular societies. A society premised on organic solidarity is composed of individuals each having a distinct job or function and their own personality; individuality flourishes as society progresses.

According to Durkheim, the more primitive a society is, the more it is subject to a mechanical solidarity and characterised by repressive laws that focus on punishment. Societies that develop according to an organic solidarity are more advanced and civilised, as their individual members become more differentiated. This type of society is characterised by restitutive law, such as civil law, constitutional and administrative law, which seek to restore relationships that have been disrupted by crime to their normal state.

In this way, law – in its approach to crime and punishment – is treated by Durkheim as a reflection of a particular society's collective morality, or its 'moral soul'. The function of punishment offers an insight into the type of society that would, for example, use boiling in oil, the rack and manacles, or picking up litter in a public place whilst wearing ankle chains and an orange jumpsuit as appropriate forms of punishment. For Durkheim, it is possible to discover what connections between law, individuality and communal interdependence are possible; and what the conditions might be for law to function as an instrument and expression of community or social solidarity, given the diverse moral composition of modem societies. His point is that as societies advance, their forms of punishment become less draconian and violent.

Be critical

Remember to consult original texts, where time and circumstances permit. An example would be Durkheim's assertion that 'the social whole always precedes the individual parts', taken from his 1893 *The Division of Labour in Society*. He uses this expression in explaining why everything, even the law, follows (or is a consequence of) the 'social'. By including quotations from a range of original sources, you will strengthen your argument and impress your tutor.

KEY THEORIST

Max Weber (1864–1920)

Max Weber rejected the 'false authority of law' thesis put forward by Karl Marx, and spoke instead of 'legitimate authority'. In his 1921 *Rechtssoziologie* ('Sociology of Law', which is a chapter in his general treatise *Wirtschaft und Gesellschaft* or 'Economy and Society'), German sociologist Max Weber's view of modern law is a means of compromise in respect of conflicting interests. He was concerned with the nature of order, viewing society as a system of structured or 'ordered action', where a particular order would claim ownership over what is deemed to be right or legitimate.

The 'rational legal order' was composed of social relations or human reciprocal 'interactions', within which (unlike 'behaviour', which is causally determined) 'meaningful' encounters take place. These meanings may not be shared by other actors who are different from each other; however, all interactions are guided by motives. The task of sociology for Weber is to uncover the motives of meaningful interaction, which he calls *Verstehen* or 'understanding'. A key motive relates to the reason(s) why people feel obliged to obey the law; the methodology relating to this research is commonly referred to as 'interpretative sociology'.

Although Weber held that the 'power to impose one's will on the behaviour of another' was responsible for reinforcing a set of norms, power is perceived as a reciprocal relationship. He proposed that there are different forms of justice or legal decisions that exert power, and these are ultimately influenced by traditions and social norms. Weber outlined two kinds of power – 'monopoly power' and 'power by authority'. In a 'monopoly power' situation, the supplier fixes the price however the buyer wants to purchase the item (mutual self-interest), whereas the ruler and the governed are both in agreement to 'power by authority'. Focus is on the meaning ascribed by both parties in the latter relationship, for it to be viewed as 'legitimate authority'. Weber outlines three types of 'ideal' legitimate authority – namely, the *traditional*, the *charismatic* and the *legal rational*.

For Weber, pivotal to the development of modern law was the formal rationalisation of law on the basis of general processes that are applied to everyone equally and fairly. To this end, he did not favour the use of judicial precedent as it was too often arbitrary, preferring modern rationalised law to be codified and therefore impersonal in its application to specific cases.

Weber's theory of authority

In his essay *The Three Types of Legitimate Rule*, published posthumously in 1958, Max Weber discussed how authority is legitimated as a belief system, and distinguished three ideal types of legitimate political leadership, domination and authority:

1. *Traditional authority* means the ability and right to rule is usually passed down, and often inherited in the case of monarchical regimes. It is legitimated by the sanctity of tradition in which maintenance of the status quo is prioritised; the system of authority is not changeable and does not support social change.

2. *Charismatic authority* originates in a leader whose mission and vision inspires, enlightens or frightens others. Followers are motivated to action because of the perceived extraordinary personality of such an individual as 'prophet' or 'sorcerer'.

3. *Legal-rational authority* is characterised by a formalistic belief in the content of the law (legal) or natural law (rationality). Obedience is not due to a particular charismatic or traditional leading authority, rather to a set of uniform principles underpinned by a (legal, political and/or economic) bureaucracy such as that evidenced in a typical modern state.

According to Weber, only the traditional and legal-rational types of authority relationships are stable enough to provide the foundations for permanent administrative structures such as legal institutions and business organisations. Structures based on charismatic authority are more precarious, since the leader derives authority only from the belief of their followers in their mission.

✓ Make your answer stand out

Weber compared and distinguished the normative science of law or jurisprudence (what *ought* to be) to the social science of law (an analysis of what *is*). You can make your answer stand out by explaining the influence he has had on Hans Kelsen in this regard; although it would be a mistake to describe Weber as a legal positivist. As Weber explains, 'Normative regulation is one important causal component of consensual action but it is not … its universal form'; Weber does not hold that everyday social action is determined or determinable according to these norms.

Be critical

In answering an essay or exam question on this topic you should explain that the sociology of law is not merely concerned with legal efficacy, rather it is a critical examination of legal effectiveness in relation to validity. For both Durkheim and Weber, law is *prima facie* a precondition of the structure of social life to be explicated within general social theory; of secondary importance is the application of general social theory to the existing legal institution. You could use examples to illustrate how, despite these similarities, each social theory leads to two very distinctive theories of law.

KEY THEORIST

Karl Marx (1818–1883)

Marx offers an alternative perspective on what is meant by law, which is placed within a wider (interdisciplinary) socioeconomic, historical and political context. He does not simply attempt to answer the question of what law *is* or *ought* to be; rather, he uses social and economic frameworks to determine the wider 'role' of law. Marx seeks to alert the oppressed classes' consciousness (the working class or proletariat) to the mystification of overall power structures and presents these actors, i.e. law and religion, as no more than simply manifestations of historical class struggle. He exposes the tools, tricks and fetishes of society's power brokers; for example, how capitalism uses law to create the myth of law's neutrality in order to propagate the notion of law's justice. In this way, law is reduced to an instrument of coercion, used by those with economic power to exploit the masses.

■ Marxist legal theory

A Marxist theory of law might be easily summarised as a materialist explanation of law as the product of class society. It is fundamentally *social*, however, because it seeks to uncover why, and with what consequences, certain social relations assume determinate legal forms. The influence of Marxism on our understanding of law hinges on its efforts to uncover the social relations expressed, mediated and obscured in such legal categories as private property, state property, constitutional governance, representative government, the general will, individual right or collective right. Opposed to natural law theory and legal positivism, the idea of right is not the property of human reason, neither is it the product of sovereign rule; rather, it is a social form of the subject, which materialises under particular historical conditions.

Marxist jurisprudence has a political and socioeconomic dimension in determining the legal institution as an ideological construct that maintains existing social relations, which are themselves based on control of the means of production. According to Soviet legal scholar, Evgeni Pashukanis, the law supports commodity-exchange theory in which even intangibles such as relationships, ideas and values can be turned into commodities, or objects that are given an arbitrary value. This means all 'transactions' are subject to the instrumental 'rules of exchange', which make no reference to the circumstances of exchange or to the characteristics of the commodities presented for exchange. In this way, social relations are reduced to mere abstractions or generalised exchange relations, as the market requires.

The ideological function of law (which legitimates the most fundamental capitalist relationship) is, therefore, hidden – as law isolates itself from the wider political economy, claiming objectivity from other disciplines and fields.

KEY DEFINITION: Marxian false consciousness

Scholars within the Marxian tradition refer to a **'false consciousness'** in which, for example, contract law assumes an equality of bargaining power; however, the reality of production relations means a manufacturer or employer is always in the most favourable position. The law as a 'mirror of inequalities in society' represents a dominant world class view in which, although tradition is an important factor, material and economic forces will always determine the evolution and content of laws.

Be critical

Critically discuss the Marxian idea of commodity fetishism in relation to legal fetishism, in order to demonstrate a deeper understanding of the relevancy of his complex theory. For Marx, commodity fetishism means that social relationships, which always occur within the context of production, are not between people as individuals but rather constitute economic relationships, as objects of exchange.

Every individual subject with distinct needs and interests enters into a relationship of equivalence with every other – which, in law, is deemed to be tantamount to equality. Modern Marxist, Evgeni Pashukanis, refers to the 'mode of substitution' in which the socially differentiated individual is replaced by the abstraction of the juridical subject or the legal person – constituting an alienated 'pure, blank individual'. Consequently, law's commitment to individuality and genuine equality, and the rights that would attach to such an autonomous person, is illusory. Marxist legal theory therefore relates to the legitimation of the capitalist state and the legal order, when 'humans are first reduced to abstractions and then dominated by their own creations'.

The illusion of objectivity makes it seem that the law stands above everything else in society, legitimising, for example, the autonomy of the judiciary and the specialisation of legal discourse – which distorts existing social relations and legal practice. This gives rise to legal fetishism, which constitutes a reversal in which individuals avow that they owe their existence to the law rather than the opposite; thereby inverting the real causal relationship between themselves and their product.

 Make your answer stand out

It is often difficult to fix the boundaries of Marxist legal theory; however, it remains a relevant and fertile area of jurisprudence. Modern scholars, such as Jürgen Habermas, Antonio Negri and Michel Foucault, Gilles Deleuze and Félix Guattari, have linked Marxism to theories of universal human rights beyond the conventional system of democratic representation. Sol Picciotto and Robert Fine have examined the problematic regulation of multinational corporations within the context of globalised capital accumulation and the classical tradition of jurisprudence respectively; whilst others, such as Catharine MacKinnon, Carol Smart and Drucilla Cornell, have related Marxism to a feminist social critique of law. It would be useful to refer to some of these modern applications in your essay.

▋ The continental tradition

A range of contemporary legal sociologists, particularly those from the continental tradition, continue to critically assess the role of law in society – for example, French philosopher Michel Foucault (1926–1984), who viewed law as an instrument of power. Rather than aiming to disclose the minimum conditions for a statement or system of statements as to 'what is law', Foucault produced a genealogy of law that examines the influence of political structures of power relations in different time periods – demonstrating the importance of historical conditions in analysing phenomena. He was concerned with the nature and function of juridical and legal power, and their essential connection to concepts of government and discipline. Dominant ideological forms of knowledge, those of the ruling class, form 'discourses of power', which in turn impose social norms enforced by regulatory institutions. For Foucault, social control is sustained by 'technologies of discipline', maintained by social institutions (such as law) that establish codes of control over human behaviour, particularly sexuality. His work is often discussed in the context of human rights and criminal law.

There are, however, many other important theorists in the sociology of law. German sociologist Niklas Luhmann (1927–1998) developed his autopoietic systems theory, which is premised on the inability of law to communicate with other social institutions because of, for example, the inflexibility of its arbitrary rules such as the binary code of guilty or innocent. Alternatively, social philosopher Jürgen Habermas (b. 1929) prioritises the communicative abilities of language, which is presumed to have a complex inner structure that allows us to regulate our communications towards achieving common goals, both at the level of an organising social system and as individuals. 'Communicative action' is considered by Habermas to be deeply consensual, as individuals coordinate their actions only on the basis of a shared understanding of goals that are inherently reasonable or worthwhile.

Pierre Bourdieu (1930–2002) views law as a social 'field' in which actors struggle for cultural, symbolic and economic capital. In so doing, objective social structures become inculcated into the subjective, intellectual experience of the actor and then develop into the reproductive professional 'habitus' of the lawyer. Bourdieu uses terms such as 'habitus' and 'juridical field' to emphasise how lawyers are socialised by organising structures and a prescribed perception of legal practices, which embed ways of knowing and acting. A diverse variety of theoretical influences exist within the sociology of law, which have distinguished the broader law and society domain.

Niklas Luhmann (1927–1998) and 'systems theory'

Luhmann holds that law is the main organising force in society; like knowledge, it is an essential, unavoidable and all-pervasive fact of the social condition. In common with politics, economics and media, law is also a 'system of communication'. Its enabling and constraining functions mean that all collective human life is directly or indirectly shaped by law. Luhmann's systems theory focuses on the normative or operational 'closure' and 'cognitive openness' of the legal system. Jurisprudence is defined as a particular variety of legal communication that constructs legal principles, responsible for ordering the juridical field, by explaining law to itself. His approach has contributed to debates between different schools of jurisprudence as to the origins of law, its character (as determinate or indeterminate) and the role of justice.

KEY DEFINITION: Autopoiesis theory

Autopoiesis means self-production. Autopoietic systems can be either biological or non-biological systems, which 'produce and reproduce [their] own elements by the interaction of its elements' – the elements that compose the system. German theorists Niklas Luhmann and Gunther Teubner both consider law to be an autopoietic social system because it is *self-organising* and *recursive*, and so produces and reproduces itself from within its own resources. There is, therefore, no law outside the law.

The fact that legal judgment arises from a closed culture, self-sustaining values and a self-referential system of legal rules does not protect it from everyday normative evaluations of justice and fairness. Also, the application of settled law to facts gives the judiciary a wide discretion and an enormous degree of autonomy. Some critics, for example Luhmann, question how positive modern law is able to fulfil its social function, and acquire legitimacy, when it is characterised by a meagre range of arbitrary rules and concepts which seem to be at odds with any underlying set of principles.

Be critical

Remember that for every strong claim there is often an equally strong counter-claim. For example, Luhmann's assertion that law is an autopoietic system (see above) is challenged by Michael Freeman in *Lloyds Introduction to Jurisprudence* (2014, 9th edition) on the grounds that law originated from somewhere; it did not just create itself from nothing. He states, 'it must have had its source in the extra-legal environment, whether this was religion, morality or power' (p. 745).

Make your answer stand out

Your essay or exam answer should demonstrate an understanding of legal reasoning as a type of knowledge production that has a tendency to increase the potential for flexibility, even inconsistency and ambiguity. A legal question, for example, may be determinate and indeterminate at the same time. It is determinate because there is an applicable legal rule and indeterminate because the judge is under no obligation to follow that rule. So, although law's contingency and complexity may compromise any claims to objectivity, it does not undermine law's legitimacy.

The indeterminacy critique of law not only presents an opportunity for exploring alternative possibilities (other contexts and fields of knowledge) in understanding the operation of law and law-making, it also justifies the classification of law as a social construction. By explaining how legal questions often lack single right answers, as well as how legal materials and methods allow for multiple outcomes in the courtroom, you will also display impressive analytical skill.

■ Putting it all together

Answer guidelines

See the essay question at the start of the chapter.

Approaching the question

You would begin by introducing the relevance of a sociological context, in that society is composed of groups or institutions that are cohesive, share common norms and have a definitive culture. Also, explain how every significant conception of law begins by addressing law as a social phenomenon that exists and acts in relation to social life. This would be followed by an introduction to this branch of jurisprudence, explaining how it arises from a variety of specific social and political theories that, in general, have two main objectives.

The first objective is to elucidate the nature and role of law from within the social environment, and the second is to explore how society's nature is expressed in and through law. It would be useful to illustrate, by referring to various theories such as those of Pound, Marx and Durkheim, the impracticality, even impossibility, of treating the law and law-making in isolation from the social source of its origins and influences. In other words, legal perspectives must be sensitive to the social settings in which they exist. ▶

Important points to include

Make sure you are familiar with and include:

- The theoretical foundations and historical development of law's symbiotic relationship with sociology

- How a diverse range of sociological traditions can be used to study and understand law

- What distinguishes sociological contributions to legal theory from others

- Arguments that underscore the claim that modern law must reflect the 'living law' in order to be legitimate

- The relationship between rights and law; also, the claim that, historically, rights are logically prior to the state and state-sanctioned laws

- The connection between law in action (the living law) and law in books; how social influences and the social environment influence the development of modern law

- The essential linkages between law and the abstract idea of the social; examples include law and the economy, law and politics, as well as law and culture

- The influence of contemporary legal sociologists in this area: for example, Roger Cotterrell, David Nelkin and Max Travers, as well as Pierre Bourdieu and Niklas Luhmann.

✓ Make your answer stand out

The sociology of law has always sought to construct more socially satisfying regulatory structures, taking into consideration the circumstances of time and place. You could mention how contemporary legal scholars are keen to address the recent changes to both law and society wrought by modern phenomena such as the 'war on terror', the global financial crisis and the effects of globalisation. It is argued by socio-legal scholars that such big issues can only be appropriately addressed by examining the underlying social processes and forces (including the diverse social networks of community) that are used to map legal demands, strategies and aspirations. Books such as *Law, Text, Terror* edited by Peter Goodrich, Lior Barshack and Anton Schulz, *Globalisation and Legal Theory* by William Twining, as well as journals such as the *Law and Society Review*, *International Journal of Law in Context* and the *Journal of Law and Society* would be useful reference sources on these topics.

READ TO IMPRESS

Banakar, R. and Travers, M. (2013) Sociological Jurisprudence, in *An Introduction to Law and Social Theory*, 2nd edition. R. Banakar and M. Travers (eds). Oxford: Hart Publishing, 35–52.

Cotterrell, R. (2005) *The Politics of Jurisprudence: A Critical Introduction to Legal Philosophy*, 2nd edition. Oxford: Oxford University Press, 145–160, 212–215.

Cotterrell, R. (2006) Law and Social Theory, in *Law, Culture and Society: Legal Ideas in the Mirror of Social Theory*. Aldershot: Ashgate, 15–32.

Deflem, M. (2008) *Sociology of Law: Visions of a Scholarly Tradition*. Cambridge: Cambridge University Press, 97–116.

Fine, R. (2002) Marxism and the Social Theory of Law, in *An Introduction to Law and Social Theory*. R. Banakar and M. Travers (eds). Oxford: Hart Publishing, 101–117.

Lacey, N. (1998) Normative Reconstruction in Socio-Legal Theory. *Social and Legal Theory*, 5(2): 131–151.

Nelkin, D. (2002) Comparative Sociology of Law, in *An Introduction to Law and Social Theory*. R. Banakar and M. Travers (eds). Oxford: Hart Publishing, 329–344.

Schluchter, W. (2003) The Sociology of Law as an Empirical Theory of Validity. *European Sociological Review*, 19(5): 537–549.

Shaw, J.J.A. (2013) Reimagining Humanities: Socio-Legal Studies in an Age of Disenchantment, in *Exploring the Socio of Socio-Legal Studies* (*Socio-Legal Studies Series*), D. Feenan (ed). Basingstoke: Palgrave Macmillan, 111–133.

www.pearsoned.co.uk/lawexpress

Go online to access more revision support, including quizzes to test your knowledge, sample questions with answer guidelines, podcasts you can download and more!

Critical legal studies

Revision checklist

Essential points you should know:

- [ ] How to distinguish the critical legal studies project (in terms of content, scope and aims) from more traditional theories of law
- [ ] The significance of law as narrative – founded on language, symbols and images
- [ ] The relationship between law and literature
- [ ] The significance of literary sources – for example, the novel and satire
- [ ] The application of literary devices, such as metaphor, in legal judgment
- [ ] The origins and importance of legal semiotics: Ferdinand de Saussure, Bernard Jackson and Peter Goodrich
- [ ] The influence of postmodern legal theory: Nietzsche, Foucault, Derrida and Lyotard
- [ ] Key themes and theorists in feminist legal theory and critical race theory

■ Topic map

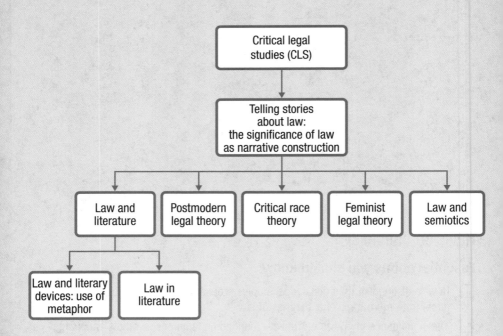

◼ Introduction

The critical legal studies project in the pursuit of law as justice: from practice to theory and ethics to aesthetics

The critical legal studies (CLS) movement challenges the accepted norms and standards that characterise legal theory and practice; it finds law neither neutral nor objective. It is further asserted that law and its claims of legitimacy rest on '**legal fictions**', which, whilst not deliberately deceptive, amount to rules established on false and inaccurate premises. CLS focuses on the relationship of legal scholarship and practice to the struggle to create a more humane, egalitarian and democratic society. Yet there is no general consensus as to methodology or core principles, only a commitment to the widest possible range of critical approaches and debate.

CLS is a relatively new jurisprudential school that began to be recognised in the United States in 1977, and can look to Marxist theories of law for its European origins. Presenting a radical alternative to more established philosophies and traditions in legal theory, its supporters offer a sceptical approach to traditional jurisprudential theories and claim that law is based on a set of political judgements, prejudices and power relationships. These are argued to comprise the hierarchical structures of domination in society that serve to legitimise injustice. For example, in the law of contractual obligations, despite the progress of doctrines of duress and undue influence along with the wider principles of unconscionability of bargains, there is still injustice and unfairness in the marketplace where a culture of individualism and unimpeded freedom to contract remains dominant.

According to the CLS mode of thought, law is not neutral or value-free but rather acts as an inescapable instrument of oppression and violence from which it is impossible to simply escape because it is integral to every form of knowledge. Often compared to the legal realists from the 1920s and 1930s, the efforts of the CLS movement are directed towards attempting to improve the legal system by urging an alignment with the social and cultural context of the law, and this means responding to modern social conditions. The strength of CLS lies in its pessimistic and critical approach to established legal phenomena, as a movement of resistance against legal doctrine.

Due to the amorphous nature of CLS, it is impossible to offer a general definition of its objectives or specific character – except to offer examples of the many interdisciplinary frames of reference (i.e. aesthetics, affect, culture, philosophy, history) and actors engaged in a sustained critique of existing legal provisions. Major influences include European philosophers, for example: nineteenth-century German social theorists Karl Marx, Friedrich Engels and Max Weber; Max Horkheimer and Herbert Marcuse of the Frankfurt School of German social philosophy; the Italian Marxist Antonio Gramsci; ▶

and poststructuralist French thinkers Michel Foucault and Jacques Derrida, who represent respectively the areas of history and literary theory. CLS also incorporates several subcategories: for example, feminist legal theory, which looks at the function of gender in the law; ecofeminism, which proposes that the oppression of women and nature are interrelated; critical race theory, which relates to the role of race in the law; postmodernism, which *inter alia* rejects historical realism and truth claims; as well as a critique of the law influenced by developments in literary theory. Contemporary critical legal scholars include Peter Goodrich, Drucilla Cornell, Costas Douzinas, Peter Fitzpatrick, Jack Balkin, Renata Salecl and Roberto Unger. Essentially they all share the same concern, namely the identification of flaws and hidden agendas in law; they also seek to identify and expose to critique the sources of marginalisation and exclusion as a vital step in mounting a response to injustice.

ASSESSMENT ADVICE

Essay questions are the chief form in evaluating your understanding of issues arising within the general context of jurisprudence, and CLS is no exception. An essay question is likely to involve a large degree of textual analysis so remember that, in CLS, language is used purposively, as a way of implying a set of meanings beyond that conveyed by any 'ordinary' understanding of the words. So it is very important that you read the question carefully, paying particular attention to the precise words (as well as the context) and what they may indicate beyond any common understanding, in order to fully ascertain what you are being asked to critically evaluate.

◼ Sample question

Could you answer this question? Below is a typical essay question that could arise on this topic. Guidelines on answering the question are included at the end of this chapter. Another sample question and guidance on tackling it can be found on the companion website.

ESSAY QUESTION

Critically assess the extent to which literature and literary devices play a significant role in the law-making and interpretative process.

■ Telling stories about law

KEY DEFINITION: Legal fictions

When a legal rule or principle is grounded on a false or inaccurate premise, we refer to this as a legal fiction. For example, the vicarious liability rule transfers responsibility from an individual to a business entity by finding the employer at fault and responsible for the actions of their employees, irrespective of any personal involvement. The owners of a company are, therefore, punished for actions they did not commit. Similarly, the claim that a liberal society under the rule of law guarantees an equal and fair society comprises a legal fiction, because inequalities of power mean that the interests and demands of certain groups (for example, those defined by class, race and/or gender) are often ignored.

We comprehend our lives in narrative form and it has been said that the heart of a lawyer is literary. Well-known contemporary legal theorists Bernard Jackson and Peter Goodrich have both referred to law as a text-based activity. In *Law, Fact, and Narrative Coherence*, Jackson argues that narrative structures have the ability to rearrange facts and law, because they inform both the content of stories and the way in which stories are told. Jackson uses various examples from legal practice to examine the experience of lawyers in the construction of narratives as they present their evidence to the court. He also demonstrates how several diverse narratives (derived from competing witness statements, the various representations of each legal team, the understanding of jury members, the judge's summary of the evidence and reasons for judgment, along with the underlying grand narratives represented by systems of doctrines and rules) comprise a hypothetical and chronological reconstruction – at the end of which each of these elements crystallise during a single trial into a particular narrative.

Each narrative supplies and constructs its own referents (discussed below in the *Legal semiotics* section), which refer back to a particular rule or legal concept and constitute the ostensible, or external, ground for a decision. The storytelling process is therefore summarised in three stages that comprise fact discovery, discovery of the law and the final stage, which involves the application of rules to the facts.

 Make your answer stand out

Consider how the law is composed of a hierarchy of texts, consequent upon events and (his-)stories played out through time. These events or dramas, such as the late nineteenth- to early twentieth-century suffragette movement (which eventually succeeded in persuading the UK government to extend the vote to all women), are part of the chronicle or story of human actions – in this case the struggle for equal participation for all in the democratic process. The historical context and terms of the ▶

Equal Franchise Act 1928 therefore constitute a key part of a general story of political emancipation. Furthermore, the limits put in place by legal authorities as a series of organising mechanisms in response to, in this instance, societal disquiet signify the fragmented nature of the relationship between legal actors and legal subjects.

The Magna Carta, A.V. Dicey's *Introduction to the Law of the Constitution* and Blackstone's *Commentaries on the Laws of England* (which he wrote after giving up an earlier career as a poet) are all examples of sacred texts that contain the story of our historical traditions and practices. These form part of the collective legal unconscious, and have contributed towards a narrative that has shaped our legal and social universe. As keeper and interpreter of such a diverse range of texts, the lawyer assumes the role of both interpreter and storyteller.

Much of what we do is communicated through the medium of language as words and expression, both written and spoken. Language has been referred to as the lawyer's scalpel, and if he is unable to use it skilfully then he is likely to butcher the case of his suffering client. A legal judgment, statute or any legal statement arranges its language as carefully, as strategically and as deliberately as does a sonnet, a novel or a theatrical performance.

The main difference between law and literature is that law involves the exercise of power in ways that literature does not; however, appreciating the value of law and literature requires us to think about the possibilities of justice and the boundaries of legal doctrine and dogma. This means acquiring an understanding of how the legal community organises and fixes these limits, which in turn demands an explication of the utility of language and linguistic devices, such as analogy, **syllogism** and metaphor, and how these are used to police and reinforce the margins of law.

Be critical

Taking a critical approach, you might explain how a law report or court case can be described as having a narrative structure, like a story. You could use an actual law report and, by referring to the headnote, the 'facts' and the 'statutes' indicated against the individual judges' interpretation of each element of the case according to their own subjective frame of reference, demonstrate how members of the judiciary privilege particular narratives over others. A judge may add their own meaning to the legal lexicon even if that meaning departs from normal or everyday language, and his or her summary of the evidence and reasons for judgment may rely on a number of differing stories and offer an idiosyncratic and distinctive adjudicatory narrative.

If we accept law as a continual story in the making, this means that law is never entirely settled or certain. Think about to what extent law's continual reassessment and transformation of its own principles throws into question the common formalist assumption relating to judicial authority – namely, that 'judges do not make law'.

▨ Law *as* literature: lawyers and literary devices

Critical legal scholars are interested in the interdisciplinary connection between law and literature, and more specifically the attribution of meaning in legal and literary texts. Understanding law *as* literature requires an examination of the language of legal texts using methods of literary interpretation with which to analyse rhetorical devices such as metaphor, analogy, hyperbole and allegory. This means that legal texts are to be read and interpreted in the same manner as literary works – as a system of narrative and dramatic prose, using techniques and vocabulary borrowed from the humanities. The justification for this exercise, according to leading academic scholars in this field such as James Boyd White, is that law is a constant process of translation from 'ordinary' language to specialised legal language and then back again. During the course of this process, important cultural and social relationships emerge that shape our social reality and define the legal landscape.

Law and metaphor

Metaphor is a pervasive feature of language, just as persuasive language is a quintessential characteristic and instrument of legal practice. By conjuring up a familiar associative image, everyday language has the ability to make the non-legal specialist audience aware of the importance of key legal concepts and decisions and so the legal profession has an enduring relationship with metaphor.

As an important figurative linguistic device, metaphor is able to ascribe a new or extended meaning of a word or phrase, which departs from its ordinary meaning. It allows us to draw comparisons and amplify a certain aspect of a particular thing and, as Aristotle states in *On Rhetoric*, it 'brings something before the eyes'. Aristotle suggested that metaphors should not be far-fetched, and were most effective when drawn from generally recognisable and similar or kindred things, so the kinship will be recognised as soon as the words are uttered. Covenants are said to 'run with the land', litigants have 'standing' and, irrespective of whether it is a higher or lower court, all judges 'sit'.

In criminal law there is mention of 'fishing expeditions', and perhaps the most well-known metaphor used by lawyers is that of 'opening the floodgates' of litigation. The power of this metaphor is illustrated by the famous 'Yorkshire Ripper' case of *Hill* v *Chief Constable for West Yorkshire* (1988) HL, which challenged the tortuous liability of statutory bodies. In this case the police failed, during their investigations of the commission of a series of similar crimes, to apprehend the perpetrator, Peter Sutcliffe. Mrs Hill claimed this amounted to negligence and a failure in their duty of care, as the criminal remained at large for a further period of time, during which he murdered the plaintiff's daughter. The invocation of the magic words 'opening the floodgates' conveyed the image of an overwhelming and uncontrollable incoming tide of complaints of negligence against the police, which would make law enforcement impossible, and so the action failed. Importantly, the public understood instantly the significance of the decision because of the evocative metaphor.

KEY EXAMPLE: Law and metaphor

In *Designers Guild Ltd.* v *Russell Williams (Textiles) Ltd.* [2000] 1 WLR 2416 at 2423, Lord Hoffman was commended for his apt reference to 'copyright law protect[ing] foxes better than hedgehogs' by Lord Fysh, who approved of this 'sibylline observation'. The metaphor comes from Isaiah Berlin's essay *The Hedgehog and the Fox*, and is an elaboration of the ancient Greek poet Archilochus' proposition, 'The fox knows many things, but the hedgehog knows one big thing'. Hoffman alluded to the ability of copyright law to offer better protection for a detailed basic idea (fox) as opposed to an indeterminate, simple and abstract idea (hedgehog), since the former was likely to indicate originality and constitute substance.

Far from being mere decoration, metaphor is one of the principal methodological devices for constructing legal principle and a necessary tool in the critique of law and legal theory. Furthermore, legal argument relies on the shrewd application of figures of speech and imagistic language, as well as the creation of myths and legal fictions on which the authority of law rests.

Be critical

You may be able to offer reasons why you believe a reliance on metaphors in judicial rhetoric may be a bad thing. Metaphors may be inappropriate, for example, and 'mixed metaphors' may lead to ambiguity and misunderstanding. They may be vague, lengthy or overused so, over time, they lose their meaning. Relating to the last point, possibly the biggest danger of relying on metaphors in judicial decision-making is that they may become a substitute for independent thought. A famous judge, Benjamin Cardozo, once remarked that metaphors in the law must be narrowly watched as they may begin as devices for liberating thought, but often end up enslaving it.

■ Law *in* literature

Often referred to as literary jurisprudence or aesthetic jurisprudence, this field of CLS encompasses a wide range of expressive mediums, including, for example, film, poetry, art, drama and music. It is a significant part of legal scholarship, which can usefully supplement legal texts, statutes, cases and commentaries. It has been said that the best way to challenge our perceptions, to make us look and think again about the law, is to call upon alternative strategies and texts. Literature works against the dulling effects of habitual deference to the stultifying structures of power, awakens the imagination and provides an alternative sentimental jurisprudence within which to contextualise and rationalise the location of the self and societal forces.

In her 1995 *Poetic Justice: The Literary Imagination and Public Life*, Martha Nussbaum writes: 'I defend the literary imagination precisely because it seems to me an essential ingredient of an ethical stance that asks us to concern ourselves with the good of other people whose lives are distant from our own.' Nussbaum makes the point that through literature we are able to understand the kind of suffering of which we have no experience, endured by people of whom we have no knowledge. Particularly through the medium of the novel, by experiencing what it feels like to participate in the lives of fictional characters at many levels of the social hierarchy, it may be possible to awaken the senses and alert these to injustice.

 Make your answer stand out

There is a great deal of law in literary works, such as the novel and classical literary texts. You might mention how CLS scholars have championed the novel as a rich source of material, which often exposes the harshness of legal doctrines and allows us to imagine a situation in advance and work out its consequences. Harper Lee's *To Kill a Mockingbird* and E.M. Forster's *Maurice* offer a privileged insight into the experiences of those who have had to endure the consequences of racial and sexual bigotry. Manuel Puig's *Kiss of the Spiderwoman* and Jeanette Winterson's *Oranges Are Not the Only Fruit* exemplify how good literature is able to evoke the lived experiences of scorned subjects and bring these to life in a variety of social, legal and political contexts.

The late sixteenth- and seventeenth-century works of William Shakespeare tend to be at the centre of literary jurisprudence, not least of all because he includes plenty of references to law and legal processes in his plays and poems. The issues and debates that trouble political and legal theorists today are the same as those that concerned Shakespearean England. His treatment of constitutional theory, for example, has enhanced our own understanding of constitutionalism. Contemporary legal theorists Ian Ward, Paul Raffield and Gary Watt have written extensively on the relationship between Shakespeare and the legal imagination, and represent useful starting points in understanding the usefulness of this jurisprudential approach. In summary, this area of jurisprudence refers to the benefits that accrue to the legal profession by engaging with certain works of literature that either centrally or peripherally confront legal issues, and in doing so enrich the cultural context of the law.

The common feature of both law and literature is language, in all of its expressive configurations. This jurisprudential approach explores the ability of narrative forms to provide insight into the nature of human experience and to better understand the role of language in explaining important legal concepts and principles.

Even constructivist theorist Ronald Dworkin, in his 1986 *Law's Empire*, speaks of the 'interpretative concept of law' as an imaginative process, in which 'The form of interpretation we are studying – the interpretation of a social practice – is like artistic interpretation in this way: both aim to interpret something created by people as an entity distinct from them'. Due to the consecutive interventions of the judges, as legal interpreters who are continually searching for the best possible result to a given case, law is similar to a never-ending story – one that creates new characters and strategies and is always in the course of writing itself in the courtroom.

 Make your answer stand out

All assessment questions on this theme will be asking you to critically analyse and justify a particular theoretical approach or frame of reference, based on a simple question or a quotation from a literary or legal source. To make your answer stand out, it is a good idea to begin with a general opening paragraph (containing a supporting reference) that suggests that critical legal scholarship finds law to be based on a hierarchical idea of knowledge and is commonly expressed through a range of techniques of separation, isolation and fear.

You could then explore the origins of those calls to acknowledge the diversity of forms of legal knowledge, which, in turn, give rise to an imperative to recognise, build connections with and promote diverse forms of practice. From this premise, you can justify the continuing relevance of the CLS approach on the basis that other jurisprudences, for example 'outsider jurisprudence' and 'minor jurisprudences', may offer a more useful and appropriate context for explicating pressing societal concerns.

■ Legal semiotics

Legal semioticians approach **legal discourse** (see page 128) from the viewpoint of their respective theories of signs and methods of creating meaning. This branch of CLS refers to the subtle influence of signs and processes of signification on the formation of legal principles and concepts. **Semiotics** (see page 125) reveals the complexity of phenomena that, whilst they seem simple on the surface, indicate beyond themselves to a wider set of meanings and are fundamentally connected to how we comprehend the world.

Legal texts and images act as signifiers, signs or symbols and mediate, or serve to explain and indicate, our shared and unique understanding of the world as a world of signs. The essential connection between the 'signifier' and the 'signified' is referred to as 'signification', and this is the process according to which meaning is constructed. So, for example, when we see an image such as *Justitia* (Lady Justice), or any statue, artwork or other representation of justice, a picture of a courtroom, police constable or a lawyer, the figure of a lawyer or a policeman, we can understand that all of these are the physical signifiers of the signified – namely that referred to as law.

Physical signifiers indicate or signify notions of authority, sovereignty, tradition and truth, and this is how a system of signs is able to wordlessly impose a set of general restrictions and prohibitions on members of society.

KEY DEFINITION: Semiotics

Semiotics refers to the role of linguistic signs in social life and how they are able to generate meaning and precede language. Ferdinand de Saussure is one of the foremost and early representatives of the movement and he emphasises the essential role of the sign in defining us by producing the subject – me and you – rather than us using language to define ourselves. In semiotic analysis, for example, a plate of food is no longer simply steak and kidney pie, chips and apple crumble; rather, it comprises a sign system that signifies matters of taste, status, class, sophistication and ethnicity.

Within CLS, **legal semiotics** is a useful frame of reference from which it is possible to explicate some of the essential issues and contentious questions arising in jurisprudence, and how these are influenced by and influence our social, cultural and political relations. It has been said that law is itself a sign, in both its content and as an institution, not least of all because it constructs human subjects as well as organisations of governance such as the courts and legislature. Furthermore, we can explicate the routine usage of various signs associated with, for example, 'law', 'legality' and 'legal practice' and how the linkages between them help to produce, maintain and modify a collectively shared interpretative framework.

KEY DEFINITION: Legal semiotics

Law is a culture that is engaged in the activity of meaning-making. Legal semiotics refers to law's language, signs and symbols and their role in structuring the legal subject, object, concepts and institutions of law. The study of legal semiotics is not concerned with the intention of these signs but their effects; similarly, it is not interested in the production of law but in its representation.

A good range of informative books and journal articles has been produced by distinguished legal semioticians, such as Bernard Jackson and Peter Goodrich, who have both written extensively on this topic. Of particular relevance are Jackson's *Semiotics and Legal Theory* and Goodrich's *Legal Discourse: Studies in Linguistics, Rhetoric and Legal Analysis* and *Languages of the Law: From Logics of Memory to Nomadic Masks*. In summary, the significance of a semiotic analysis of legal language lies in its attempts to reveal the (often hidden) political, psychological and social functions of legal language.

It is important that key terms and phrases are precisely explicated and properly applied. Critical legal theorists often employ initially unfamiliar vocabulary and idiom, and it may take a while to become accustomed to their more nuanced manner of expression. One word may have a range of diverse and subtly different meanings, sometimes depending on the context of application.

Use an encyclopaedia to research expressions such as deconstruction, discourse and critique; there is a variety of such sources on the Internet. Then, when you read these terms or phrases in context, you will understand what a particular legal scholar is attempting to explain; also, remember that they may be used in a dissimilar way by individual writers.

! Don't be tempted to . . .

Don't rely on just one reference source; there is a vast range of materials in this subject area. You will also find that certain ideas, texts and writers are easier to read than others. If you feel you have not grasped or understood a particular writer, issue or theory, find a secondary text such as a journal article or book chapter that discusses that particular theory or idea. You will find materials in the library or via the Internet that discuss the same topic or theorists in a more easily digestible manner, or in a way that appeals to your own mode of understanding.

■ Postmodern legal theory

Friedrich Nietzsche, Michel Foucault, Jacques Derrida, Jean-François Lyotard and Jacques Lacan comprise some of the key postmodern philosophers who have influenced the development of critical legal theory. A common theme is the **deconstruction** of the **metanarratives** (comprehensive totalising explanations) according to which those in power would seek to 'write' or dictate the conditions under which the rest of us should live.

Primarily by using language (textual analysis), postmodernist legal theorists seek to prioritise individual agency (autonomy), and a corollary of this is social diversity – with a respect for difference at its core. In his seminal work, *The Postmodern Condition*, published in 1979, Lyotard suggested that postmodernism was committed to the ideas of social and political reform. His idea of '*differend*' (in the sense of dispute) was preserved by language, the language of resistance. For Nietzsche, individuals flourish best under 'conditions of disorder', having asserted themselves against the repressive rule of the prescribed order. In this way he equates the idea of disorder or dissent with freedom and agency.

For postmodernists, language (the unmasking of 'truth' narratives and narratives of power, for example) is at the heart of their commitment to address the question of justice; whilst at the same time resisting the centralised force of law as the, non-legitimate, 'mystical foundations of authority'.

KEY DEFINITION: Deconstruction

The idea of deconstruction is a postmodernist, Derridean idea that arises from the premise that there is always more to the text than that which is written by the author; this additional information is provided by the context of the text and the context of the reader. Determinable ideas that ground law and legal principle, such as tradition, history, binary oppositions such as innocent/guilty and concepts such as the 'criminal', are viewed as malleable, 'mystical' and 'imaginary' constructs of power. It is upon these constructs that modern law depends in order to exert control over individuals in society. However, for deconstructionists, legal texts (statutes and case law) and principles are never 'closed off' to other possible interpretations; they cannot fix 'meaning', as the reader will always introduce their own context and, in so doing, rewrite the text.

For Derrida, law is an expression of power relations, whilst justice is a matter of ethics that relates to each individual situation according to its unique properties. Against traditional theories of jurisprudence, postmodernist legal theory deconstructs their inherent universalism, privileging of 'reason', conceptual knowledge and concern with the past; rather, they focus on the particular politics that constitutes a specific context or situation in the present – whilst hoping to empower the potential for future change.

The postmodern project is irreducibly political; it demands political and legal recognition of the 'Other' (Emmanuel Lévinas, Jacques Derrida) in terms of their 'otherness'. This would include all those in Western society who are considered to be 'outsiders', such as women, the elderly, black and ethnic minorities, the LGBTQ community and the disabled. The ability to participate in the construction of rules and the interpretation of law becomes, then, dependent on a communicative relation – having a voice, being recognised as a differentiated individual – in which case, at the simplest level, realising justice is simply a matter of conversation.

▊ Feminist legal theory

Feminist legal thought relates to a wider debate on sameness and difference. For example, criminal law assumes all 'criminals' are the same in the sense that, within their categories, all crimes are the same and conform to certain shared characteristics. This approach assumes that important distinctions between people of different ethnic, racial and social groups are not real differences, and this idea is often detrimental to their interests. In the case of women and criminal law, there is an added gender disadvantage. Many laws subscribe to the particular fiction about the 'nature' of women (comprising the restrictive 'normative woman') as objects of support or oppression according to gendered legal contexts. The crime of infanticide based on the assumption that maternal (as opposed to paternal) killings are a result of postpartum psychosis – feminist legal theorists use this as another example of over-gendering and, significantly, conforming to a stereotype of the 'mad woman'. In this way deviance is linked to reproductive difference and the individual woman's experience is decontextualised and depoliticised.

There is a diverse range of views composing feminist legal theory. Scholars such as Carol Smart, Catharine MacKinnon, Judith Butler and Drucilla Cornell have all written books and papers that challenge gender disadvantage and the social and cultural construction of sex and gender within law and the legal profession.

KEY DEFINITION: Legal discourse

Legal discourse refers to law's language (as text and speech) as a distinctive communicative form that has both a prescriptive and normative character. The written codes and textual accounts of the judicial process produce a wide-ranging legal discourse. This is generally defined as the 'language of law', as applied within its social and ideological context and as understood by reference to the 'discursive' practices of the legal community.

Often the term 'legal language' is used interchangeably with 'legal discourse' but the latter is more accurate and indicates the specific contexts and relationships implicated in, for example, the hierarchical and historically produced uses of language. Legal discourse encapsulates the various relationships between language use and the realm of law, and is commonly analysed from within the context of, for example, legal theory, philosophy, semiotics and formal logic.

Critical race theory

Critical race theorists (CRT) argue that legal guarantees of equality and 'justice for all' have not materialised for the non-dominant groups in society, who have suffered a long history of slavery, segregation, subordination and continuing exclusion. Although the law purports to be neutral and colour-blind, CRT challenges these legal fictions by finding liberalism and democracy as a vehicle for the self-interest, power and privilege of the dominant classes in society – which are identified as straight, male and white. Unlike civil rights scholars, critical race theorists focus on the broader social conditions of racial inequality – analysing the development of law through the history, experiences and racial sensibilities of racial minorities.

The historical and cultural analyses of race and racism of, for example, Richard Delgado, Mari Matsuda and Jean Stefancic, draw primarily upon the experiences of minorities in the United States, although recent CRT scholarship has extended to calls for the reform of international law and institutions.

■ Putting it all together

Answer guidelines

See the sample question at the start of the chapter.

Approaching the question

This branch of jurisprudence engages with all forms (text and image) of narrative expression, in articulating the demands of justice against the arbitrary exercise of power. In composing your answer, you will begin by outlining what is meant by 'literature'. Figurative literary devices permeate legal rhetoric, legal judgments and core legal principles. You can refer to the use of analogy and metaphor, and provide examples of the contexts in which they occur, such as use of the term 'floodgates'. Equitable maxims such as 'he who comes to equity must come with clean hands' constitute a powerful visual indication of the need for a clean conscience to protect the integrity of the court. Aside from its obvious gender bias, visual legal constructs such as the 'reasonable man' help to create a certain attitude towards the concept to which it refers – which may or may not coincide with the 'ordinary' understanding of this expression. So, your answer will illustrate both the ubiquitous nature of literary devices, and their influence on legal and popular opinion.

You could then address the importance of references to law and the fictional lived consequences of legal rules and sanctions within such aesthetic forms as the novel, the play and poem, and by extension in art and music. We can learn much from these dramatic contexts: for example, Charles Dickens' *Bleak House* and Nelle Harper Lee's *To Kill a Mockingbird* both exemplify complex moral and legal dilemmas arising from human experience. You might also mention the significance of semiotics to law: how law can be understood as a system of signs, underpinned by processes of signification, expression, representation and communication. Due to its complexity and often opaque language, discussing this theory would be a more arduous, intellectually challenging, though ultimately rewarding pursuit.

Important points to include

- ■ Explain the commonalities between law and literature, how law is a text-based exercise in narrative construction and is, therefore, similar to conventional storytelling.

- ■ Use analogical reasoning, by comparing the courtroom to the scene of a drama in which each person plays a part, from the presiding judge right down to the witnesses. You could illustrate this proposition by reference to a particular law report; show how it tells a story, beginning with the case headnote, which sets ▶

out the facts and relevant statute, to the individual judgments that represent a distinctive narrative interpretation according to the predispositions and influences exhibited by each individual judge.

■ This is an interdisciplinary area and some tutors will tend to focus on favourite literary sources: for example, Dickens has been used by Martha Nussbaum and Shakespeare by Ward and Raffield to critique modern law, justice and constitutionalism.

■ Discuss and give examples of how the novel has often been deployed as a means of depicting law as an ordering mechanism in society, also often as a vehicle of injustice.

■ Give examples of literary sources used in judicial rhetoric. In a famous US Supreme Court case, *Plaut* v *Spendthrift Farm Inc* (1995) 514 U.S. 211, Justice Scalia quoted, from Robert Frost's poem *Mending Wall*, the aphorism 'Good fences make good neighbours' to support his view on the separation of powers. A similar example of rhetorical persuasion was given by Lord Justice Wall, who quoted from Philip Larkin's famous poem *This Be The Verse* in a postscript to his judgment (concerning an acrimonious residence application) in *R (A Child)* [2009] EWCA Civ 358, as a warning to warring parents of the serious consequences their fighting was likely to have on the child.

 ## Make your answer stand out

You will make your answer stand out in this area by referring to relevant theories and theorists who exemplify the points you make in your arguments. For example, if you are talking about the significance of the use of imagery and symbols in law and support your answer by referring to the work of Peter Goodrich or Bernard Jackson, this will impress your examiners. Similarly, if you are writing about the relevance of literature to lawyers, you could refer to the writings of satirist Jonathan Swift (who wrote *Gulliver's Travels*) and explain how these have been used to highlight the need for social reform. Such supporting references will make a good impression.

Referring to original sources to illustrate your answer, even mentioning some of the core ideas of, for example, Levinas or Derrida in relation to the appropriate field of inquiry, will earn extra marks. Often it may be difficult to locate good quotations or a sentence expressing a key idea within the sections of a long text, so learn to identify key words/expressions and the names of key thinkers and look for these in the reference section at the back of a particular book.

To achieve good grades in jurisprudence, you need to use language precisely and cogently, and try to improve your vocabulary by reading as much as you can. Remember, a good lawyer is essentially a wordsmith with excellent writing and presentation skills, albeit one who writes for a rarefied audience within a particular context.

READ TO IMPRESS

Ben-Dor, O. (2011) Introduction: standing before the gates of law, in *Law and Art: Justice, Ethics and Aesthetics*. Abingdon: Routledge, 1–29.

Boyd White, J. (1999) Writing and Reading in Philosophy, Law and Poetry, in *Law and Literature: Current Legal Issues* Volume 2, M. Freeman and A. Lewis (eds). Oxford: Oxford University Press, 1–21.

Cover, R.M. (1983) The Supreme Court 1982 Term – Foreword: Nomos and Narrative. *Harvard Law Review*, 97: 4–68.

Dolin, K. (2011) *A Critical Introduction to Law and Literature*. Cambridge: Cambridge University Press, 1–16, 19–40.

Douzinas, C. and Nead, L. (1999) *Law and the Image: The Authority of Art and the Aesthetics of Law*. Chicago: University of Chicago Press, 1–35.

Goodrich, P. (1990) *Languages of Law: From Logics of Memory to Nomadic Masks*. London: Weidenfeld & Nicolson, 11–148, 209–259.

Jackson, B. (2010) *Prospects of Legal Semiotics*, A. Wagner and J.M. Broekman (eds). Dordrecht: Springer, 3–37.

MacKinnon, C.A. (2002) Keeping it Real: On anti-'essentialism', in *Crossroads, Directions, and a New Critical Race Theory*, F. Valdes, J. McCristal Culp and A.P. Harris (eds). Philadelphia: Temple University Press, 71–86, 411–412.

Manderson, D. (2000) Prelude: Senses and Symbols in Aesthetic Experience, in *Songs Without Music: Aesthetic Dimensions of Law and Justice*. Berkeley: University of California Press, 3–24.

Nussbaum, M.C. (1995) *Poetic Justice: The Literary Imagination and Public Life*. Boston, MA.: Beacon Press, xiii–xix, 1–12.

Raffield, P. (2010) *Shakespeare's Imaginary Constitution: Late Elizabethan Politics and the Theatre of Law*. Oxford: Hart Publishing, 1–50, 153–181.

Shaw, J.J.A. (2012) The Continuing Relevance of Ars Poetica to Legal Scholarship and the Modern Lawyer. *International Journal for the Semiotics of Law*, 25(1): 71–93.

Ward, I. (2004) *Introduction to Critical Legal Theory*. Abingdon: Routledge-Cavendish, 155–182.

Ward, I. (2009) *Law, Text, Terror*. Cambridge: Cambridge University Press, 1–26, 178–192.

www.pearsoned.co.uk/lawexpress

 Go online to access more revision support, including quizzes to test your knowledge, sample questions with answer guidelines, podcasts you can download and more!

And finally, before the exam . . .

Having read through the various chapters in this book you should now be in a position to understand that the concerns of jurisprudence are much the same as those that arise in both a legal context and from within wider society, which means there is an inherent connection between the law and the social sciences. Since legal concepts are formulated by, and imposed upon, particular communities of people (those who make the law and those who are subject to, and objects of, the law), the arts and humanities also relate to law. History and language, for example, are important since law's legitimacy rests on the transmission of its ancient traditions, and relies on both the text (cases and statutes) and image (visual metaphors, court etiquette and forms of dress) from which it derives its identity and authority.

Just remember that although jurisprudence is considered to be a difficult subject area, by acquiring a philosophical understanding of some of the most commonly used legal principles, you will better understand the nature, function, purpose and possibilities of law. This also means you will become a better law student, legal scholar or practising lawyer.

Check your progress

- [ ] Look at the **revision checklists** at the start of each chapter. Are you happy that you can now tick them all? If not, go back to the particular chapter and work through the material again. If you are still struggling, seek help from your tutor.
- [ ] Attempt the **sample questions** in each chapter and check your answers against the guidelines provided.
- [ ] Go online to www.pearsoned.co.uk/lawexpress for more hands-on revision help:
    - [ ] Try the **test your knowledge** quizzes and see if you can score full marks for each chapter.
    - [ ] Attempt to answer the **sample questions** for each chapter within the time limit and check your answers against the guidelines provided.

▶

☐ Listen to the **podcast** and then attempt the question it discusses.

☐ Evaluate sample exam answers in **you be the marker** and see if you can spot their strengths and weaknesses.

☐ Use the **flashcards** to test your recall of the key theories and theorists you've revised and the definitions of important terms.

■ Linking it all up

Although key theories in jurisprudence can be studied as discrete entities, according to their distinct core features, there are many legal concepts and contemporary issues that are best understood by comparing the merits of one jurisprudential theory against another. Legal theories may be applied to topics as diverse as the traditional – what is the appropriate content for the rule of law, to the less conventional – adoption of children by same-sex couples.

If you can successfully identify and critically analyse the pertinent aspects of one theory or theorist against a competing theory or perspective, in relation to appraising a legal concept or contemporary issue, this will greatly enhance your academic performance and increase your mark significantly. Here are some examples of key areas where a comparative analysis is useful, if not essential:

✔ Asking the fundamental 'law question' – in other words, what is the nature, purpose and role of law in society – requires we compare contrasting theories and theorists. The core features of two mainstream, well-established legal theories, 'natural law' and 'legal positivism', are outlined in Chapters 4 and 5, respectively, and are the usual starting point for arguing the merits and demerits of this big question.

✔ Critical legal theorists – introduced in Chapter 8 – offer a critical or censorious perspective on law, often viewing law as legitimised violence and a mechanism for the arbitrary control and coercion of individual behaviour. As the newest movement in jurisprudence, their critique of law's formalism and indeterminacy can be traced to American legal realism – discussed in Chapter 6.

✔ In all theoretical positions offered within the context of jurisprudence, the focus is on the language of law and the legitimate use of 'sovereign' or ruling power. How key terms such as autonomy, right, justice, fairness and morality are understood and applied by various theorists illustrates the wider role language plays in constructing foundational legal rules and concepts – which are, in turn, used to legitimate the enforcement of law in society.

■ Knowing your key theories, theorists and approaches

Make sure you know how to use relevant theories, theorists and a variety of interdisciplinary approaches to understanding the wider scope of law and law-making to support your answers. Use the table below to focus your revision of the key examples in each topic. To review the details of these, refer back to the particular chapter.

Key example (theory, theorist or theme)	Approaching the topic	Related topics
Chapter 1 – The nature and scope of jurisprudence		
Understanding the purpose of jurisprudence	Demonstrate the usefulness of adopting a theoretical approach to reading the law	Analysing legal concepts, principles and attitudes from a variety of critical perspectives
Distinguishing between an analytical versus a normative approach to law	It is necessary to show you have grasped the basic difference between the analytical approach, which is concerned with describing the content of legal rules, as against the normative approach – adherents of which purport to understand the law as it stands and, rather, critically evaluate what the law *ought* to be	These contrasting approaches are evidenced in the hard positivist v. natural law positions, although there are areas of overlap
The main schools of jurisprudence all share a similar obsession with vocabulary and the use of rarefied/ complex language	Understand the importance of language to legal theorists; key terms and expressions are rarely used according to their 'ordinary' meaning	Regarding all schools of jurisprudence, it is necessary to become familiar with the way in which legal theorists explicate favourite expressions and use these to critique the law

▶

Key example (theory, theorist or theme)	Approaching the topic	Related topics
Chapter 2 – Rights and justice		
The importance of distinguishing legal rights from moral rights	Remember, legal rights are based on existing legal rules, written down, for example, in statute and case law. Moral rights are a matter of belief and values and are, therefore, often contested	This fundamental distinction forms the basis for much debate between legal theorists
The will theory approach (Kant, Savigny, Hart, Kelsen, Wellman, Steiner)	Understand how will theory explains that the right-holder is a small-scale sovereign, who has absolute control over another person's duties, on the basis of human agency and the capacity for freedom	Interest theory
The interest theory approach (Bentham, Austin, Lyons, MacCormick, Raz)	Understand how interest theory maintains that the right-holder has a right to further their best interests, which are allied to the social and biological prerequisites for leading a minimally good life	Will theory
Main approaches to the idea of justice (Kant, Rawls, Nozick)	Jurisprudence is concerned with law as justice. Although justice itself has no substantive content, it is an interpretative concept that is underscored by a range of important theories	Distributive justice, procedural justice, utilitarianism and libertarianism
John Rawls' original position and veil of ignorance	Assumption of the 'original position' of free and equal individuals, committed to principles of social and political justice, demands impartiality of judgement. This requires all knowledge of the personal features, social and historical circumstances must be concealed behind a 'veil of ignorance'	Distributive justice

Key example (theory, theorist or theme)	Approaching the topic	Related topics
Chapter 3 – Law and morality		
Immanuel Kant's categorical imperative	The belief that humans must choose impartially conceived moral maxims (or reasons given for legitimating a certain action) that apply to everyone, in the same circumstances, without contradiction or exception	Moral philosophy, deontology, the idea of human agency
Lon Fuller's 'inner morality of law'	Demonstrate his support for the idea that law ought to be made in accordance with eight criteria, comprising a minimum standard that embodies the moral requirements of consistency and fairness	*Hart* v *Fuller* debate
Lord Patrick Devlin and the 'enforcement of morality'	Be familiar with the reasons Devlin insists that the protection of morals (as understood and accepted by a majority of the public) is to be prioritised above the protection of individual freedom	*Hart* v *Devlin* debate, the Wolfenden Report
Chapter 4 – Classical and modern natural law		
Thomas Aquinas' classical natural law theory	The starting point for understanding Aquinas' theory is that the law (as necessarily moral) is derived from the nature of the world, and humans who are created in God's image and so are capable of reason	Deontology, Kant's moral philosophy
John Finnis' modern natural law theory	You need to understand how Finnis' theory shares some ideas with, yet departs from, deontological natural law theory – being based on the idea that humans have a moral aim that is a 'common' need for certain basic goods	Against the idea of Hume's practical reason, Aquinas' and Kant's theory of natural law

▶

Key example (theory, theorist or theme)	Approaching the topic	Related topics
Consequentialism	You need to be able to understand what makes a theory consequentialist. Consequentialists maintain that choices that inform our actions or intentions are morally evaluated solely by the end results or outcomes	Deontology
Deontology	You need to appreciate that, for deontologists, the 'right reason' for an action is their main consideration; such a moral motivation is completely separated from any consequences. So, for example, if telling lies is morally wrong, then lying is without exception *always* immoral, even if a lie might save someone's life	Consequentialism, deontological ethics

Chapter 5 – Classical and modern legal positivism

The separability thesis	It is important to grasp this idea, which is central to the main varieties of positivism – namely, that there is no 'necessary' connection between law and morality	H.L.A. Hart's legal positivism, against natural law theory
The sources thesis	You need to understand that this theory claims the existence and content of law can always be determined by reference to its sources without recourse to moral argument. Sources include not just legal judgments and statutes, but also the circumstances of promulgation	Joseph Raz's (hard) positivism

Key example (theory, theorist or theme)	Approaching the topic	Related topics
Utilitarianism	It is important to appreciate this important (consequentialist) theory, which is based on the idea that happiness, as the greatest good for the greatest number of people, is the proper end of human action – as it is nothing more than the aggregate of individual human interests	Jeremy Bentham, John Stuart Mill
Hans Kelsen's 'pure theory of law'	You need to understand Kelsen's project to develop a 'legal science' in which a 'system of norms' would provide a hierarchy of all laws, and particularly map the origins of foundational laws from which all others derive. The fact that Kelsen's 'basic norm' or *Grundnorm* validates all lower norms would obviate the necessity to trace its origins to a superhuman source, such as those indicated by moral theories of law	H.L.A. Hart, Joseph Raz
Ronald Dworkin's 'right answer' thesis	You need to demonstrate an understanding of the reasons for Dworkin's general anti-positivist position and his more specific criticisms of H.L.A. Hart's theory. Against Hart's idea that judges can use their discretion in 'hard cases' when legal sources are exhausted, show how Dworkin's objective 'right answer' thesis suggests the methods of legal argumentation extend to finding the law in moral facts – as all legal principles relate to the realm of morality. The ideal judge has an obligation to find the right answer, because one of the parties always has a right to win	H.L.A. Hart's rule of recognition, law and morality, rights and justice

►

Key example (theory, theorist or theme)	Approaching the topic	Related topics
Chapter 6 – Legal realism		
Legal realism: the approach to understanding law as it *really* is	You need to understand that legal realists (both the Scandinavian and American theorists) are keen to try and explicate the law as it really is. To this end, both attempt to explain law in terms of observable behaviour (analysing cause and effect) and are sceptical about values such as justice and right, as well as being suspicious of metaphysical explanations	Oliver Wendell Holmes Jr, Karl Llewellyn
Oliver Wendell Holmes' prediction theory of law	You need to appreciate Holme's central thesis, which is of great significance to American legal realists generally. Law is presented as mere 'prophecies of what the courts will do in fact'. This involves viewing law from the point of view of a 'bad man' who is not concerned with acting morally or in accordance with a grand philosophical scheme. Rather, the focus is on whether and to what degree certain acts will incur punishment or other court sanction	American legal realism, the indeterminacy thesis, Karl Llewellyn's 'law jobs' theory
The indeterminacy thesis	You need to appreciate this important concept, which claims judges may decide cases by taking into consideration factors other than pre-existing law – for example, relying on personal bias or intuition – which renders law indeterminate or unknowable/ uncertain	Oliver Wendell Holmes Jr's prediction theory of law

Key example (theory, theorist or theme)	Approaching the topic	Related topics
The Scandinavian legal realist approach	You need to be able to distinguish the Scandinavian legal realists, who were more interested in philosophical questions about the nature of law and how to locate it within the natural law of physical sciences. They were more interested in the theoretical operation of the legal system as a whole and were hostile to all modes of conceptual thinking, which they viewed as metaphysical or ideological	Axel Hägerström, Anders Vilhelm Lundstedt, Alf Ross, as distinct from American legal realism

Chapter 7 – Sociological jurisprudence

Appreciating the value of a sociological approach to law	You should be able to explain the significance of examining the social effects of legal institutions, doctrines and practices and, conversely, the influence of social phenomena on both substantive and procedural aspects of law-making	The influence of Montesquieu's *De l'esprit des lois*, Durkheim, Weber, Marx, Luhmann and Foucault
Roscoe Pound's theory of interests	You need to understand the core idea of this theory, which relates to the possibility of balancing individual, social and public interests. Law needs to find a balance in maximising all such interests; however, Pound's 'theory of interests' aims to help determine which interests have priority	(Consequence-based theory) pragmatism, social interests theory (pluralism)

▶

Key example (theory, theorist or theme)	Approaching the topic	Related topics
Émile Durkheim's mechanical solidarity and organic solidarity	You need to understand how, for this prominent social theorist, law is the most visible symbol of social solidarity and the organisation of social life. Mechanical solidarity produces repressive laws that prioritise a collective consciousness, focusing on control and punishment; whilst organic solidarity is characterised by an evolving society of individuals governed by restitutive laws that seek to restore relationships and work through lawyers and the courts	Collectivism, individualism
Luhmann's systems theory	You need to understand the contribution of Luhmann to legal scholarship in his construction of a complex new paradigm for comparing legal systems to other social systems	Niklas Luhmann, Gunther Teubner, Jürgen Habermas, autopoietic social systems theory

Chapter 8 – Critical legal studies

Understanding the critical legal studies (CLS) project	You need to appreciate that the CLS movement is still relatively new and is less formal than other schools of jurisprudence, being organised around a wide range of interdisciplinary approaches and topical, sometimes controversial, issues. Essentially, critical legal theorists seek to improve the legal system by urging an alignment with the social and cultural context of the law, and this means responding to modern social conditions	Postmodernist legal theory, critical race theory, queer theory, feminist legal theory, literary approaches to law

Key example (theory, theorist or theme)	Approaching the topic	Related topics
Law's language	You need to be able to explain how law – being premised on the spoken word (performed in court, for example) and text (statutes, case reports) – uses language in specific ways to legitimise its activities and coerce certain forms of behaviour	Legal hermeneutics, law and literature, James Boyd White, Peter Goodrich. Ronald Dworkin, in *A Matter of Principle*, describes a legal text as 'a literary work produced by many authors'
The importance of legal fictions and language games	You need to understand the role of language games in coercing individual actions and justifying legal rules. The construction of legal fictions (convenient legal untruths) is a significant means of legitimising propositions about the substance or procedures of the legal system. An example is constitutional legitimacy, which rests on the notion of 'consent of the governed', which is an impossible standard; however, this ideal of popular sovereignty creates an impression of fair play that obliges obedience to laws with or without consent	Law and persuasive literary devices, law and metaphor, law and analogy, legal semiotics
Postmodern legal theory	You need to be able to explain postmodern legal theory as a critical analysis of inequalities and injustices relating to, for example, gender, class, race and ethnicity. Deconstruction is one interpretative method by which theorists have critically engaged with diversity and multiplicity – in order to acknowledge the widest possible range of diverse behaviours and values	The writings of Friedrich Nietzsche, Michel Foucault, Jacques Derrida, Jean-François Lyotard and Jacques Lacan

■ Sample question

Below is an essay question that incorporates competing areas of the law. See if you can answer this question, drawing upon your knowledge of the whole subject area. Guidelines on answering this question are included at the end of this section.

ESSAY QUESTION

Jurisprudence is the theory or philosophy of law. It addresses the nature of law and justice, origins and authority of the state, the relationship between law and morality and, importantly, the legitimate scope of legal authority. The relationship between law and language is also significant, not only in developing legal discourse but also, more generally, in the formulation of key legal concepts and principles on which the law-making process depends.

Explain why jurisprudence is still relevant today, with reference to key legal theories.

Answer guidelines

Approaching the question

The question begins by outlining some of the main tasks of legal theorists in addressing the nature, scope and function of law. As it covers the whole spectrum from traditional classical theories to modern critical expositions, you are invited to choose key formative elements of the entire scope of jurisprudential inquiry to illustrate the continuing utility of jurisprudence. In composing your answer, you should first explain why the ideas (those big questions relating to the role of morality, for example, the recognition of rights, law as justice) explored by classical legal theorists throughout history are still relevant today. Ideally you would end your essay by addressing the CLS school of jurisprudence and its focus on contemporary legal dilemmas and diverse rights claims that often perplex lawyers.

Important points to include

- An introduction that shows the range and diversity of classical and modern theories of jurisprudence.
- Discussion of the core principles from within the range of jurisprudential theories and the relative importance given to these key concepts by different theorists. Be sure to compare approaches to these ideas, emphasising the nature of jurisprudence as essentially argumentative.

- You could make reference to key contemporary theorists on core themes from a particular school of jurisprudence, and illustrate how each tends to follow in the tradition of earlier scholarship.
- Finally, explain why areas of conflict have arisen and how the same big questions are still pertinent and fertile topics of jurisprudential debate in modern times.

 Make your answer stand out

- You could also acknowledge the potential of jurisprudence to address a diverse range of societal problems in relation to the role of a modern legal institution in acknowledging and overcoming these.
- You could suggest how jurisprudence is able to offer a critical perspective on contemporary subjects as diverse as mitigating the diasporic consequences of globalisation by developing appropriate international human rights laws, appropriately fixing the boundaries of terror legislation, to 'outsider jurisprudence' – discussing, for example, how to protect the rights of transgender persons in relation to having their new identities registered on official documentation such as passports.
- You need to demonstrate an understanding of not only key theories and typical theorists but also unfamiliar expressions (which acknowledge the deliberate technicality and complexity of legal language), and use a good range of illustrative quotations to support your assertions.
- Finally, jurisprudence is not a descriptive subject where simply offering a 'bottom line' explanation is enough; you need to show interpretative and comparative legal skills.
- In order to really impress your tutor and examiners and get the very best marks, you need to read widely, preferably with enthusiasm, and in so doing cultivate the ability to express your thoughts and findings expertly, eloquently and with precision.

Further practice

To test yourself further, try to answer these three questions, which also incorporate overlapping areas of the law. Evaluate your answers using the answer guidelines available on the companion website at **www.pearsoned.co.uk/lawexpress**

Question 1

On the question of legal interpretation, according to H.L.A. Hart's positivist model of law, what determines the areas of 'core' and 'penumbra' in rule making?

Question 2

Lord Sumption, Justice of the UK Supreme Court, recently stated 'The attraction of judge-made law is that it appears to have many of the virtues which the political process inevitably lacks. It is transparent. It is public. Above all, it is animated by a combination of abstract reasoning and moral value-judgment'. Critically analyse this statement.

Question 3

Discuss the extent to which the critical legal studies movement has been successful in 'relating legal scholarship and practice to the struggle to create a more humane, egalitarian and democratic society' (Kennedy and Klare, 1984, p. 461).

Glossary of terms

The glossary is divided into two parts: key definitions and other useful terms. The key definitions can be found within the chapter in which they occur as well as in the glossary below. These definitions are the essential terms that you must know and understand in order to prepare for an exam. The additional list of terms provides further definitions of useful terms and phrases that will also help you answer examination and coursework questions effectively. These terms are highlighted in the text as they occur but the definition can only be found here.

■ Key definitions

Analytical jurisprudence Analytical (or sometimes referred to as 'analytic') jurisprudence has been described, by John Austin, as the study of the nature of law only at its most general and abstract level. Although its boundaries are not clearly defined, it is concerned with the formal analysis of concepts and seeks to analyse law and legal constructs from a neutral viewpoint, according to the key facets. Analytical theory asks such questions as 'what *is* the law?' and 'what is the relationship between law and morality?' at a descriptive level.

Aquinas' nature of law Aquinas divided natural law into four distinct types:

- *Lex Aeterna* (Eternal Law): timeless laws that apply to the 'whole community of the universe' and are governed by God, including physical (scientific, biological, etc.) laws as well as God's plan for the universe – without which people would lack direction;

- *Lex Divina* (Divine Law): law revealed by scripture and divine revelation and not by human reason;

- *Lex Naturalis* (Natural Law): that part of eternal law, governing rational behaviour and free will, that is discoverable by reason;

- *Lex Humana* (Human Law): supported by human reason and articulated via human authorities for the common good; a human law is only valid if it conforms to the content or general principles of natural law.

GLOSSARY OF TERMS

Autopoiesis theory

Autopoiesis means self-production. Autopoietic systems can be either biological or non-biological systems, which 'produce and reproduce [their] own elements by the interaction of its elements'. German theorists Niklas Luhmann and Gunther Teubner both consider law to be an autopoietic social system because it is self-organising and recursive, and so produces and reproduces itself from within its own resources. There is, therefore, no law outside the law.

Consequentialism

Consequentialists hold that the consequences of human action form the basis for any judgement concerning the rightness of that conduct, so a morally right act (or omission) is one that will produce a good outcome, or consequence.

Deconstruction

The idea of deconstruction is a postmodernist, Derridean idea that arises from the premise that there is always more to the text than what is written by the author; this additional information is provided by the context of the text and the context of the reader. Determinable ideas in law such as tradition, history, binary oppositions such as innocent/guilty and concepts such as the 'criminal' are viewed as malleable, 'mystical' and 'imaginary' constructs of power. It is upon these constructs that modern law depends in order to exert control over individuals in society. However, for deconstructionists, legal texts (statutes and case law) and principles are never 'closed off' to other possible interpretations; they cannot fix 'meaning', as the reader will always introduce their own context and, in so doing, rewrite the text.

Deontological

Deontological moral theories come in a variety of forms, but the main thrust is the concept of duty and the rightness of action (making the correct moral choices) in relation to a moral rule as to whether the action is morally required, forbidden or permitted. Kant's theory of moral philosophy is considered deontological because, first, people must act in a morally virtuous way from duty (rather than desire) and, secondly, only the motives of the actor make the action moral, not the outcome of the action.

Devlin's concept of moral legalism

Devlin rejected the distinction between public and private morality, claiming that the protection of morals in the public interest is more powerful than the protection of the individual freedom of consenting parties in an immoral act. To this end, he proposed three guiding principles that would enable the interests of private individuals to be balanced against the public requirements of society:

■ Law should support a maximum standard of individual freedom as far as compatible with social integrity.

- Law should only intervene when society, the 'right-minded' citizenry, refuses to tolerate certain behaviour.
- Privacy should be respected, but those interests must be balanced with the need for law to be enforced in the face of internal or external threats.

Distributive justice

Distributive justice relates to the development of normative principles that can lead to the fair or socially just distribution of goods – for example, power, wealth, reward, privileges and respect – according to the merits of the individual and the best interests of society.

Ehrlich's 'living law'

For Ehrlich, the 'living law' has enormous influence because it goes beyond the confines of statute and judgment, by regulating all social life and producing social norms or norms of behaviour that govern all social relations.

Empiricism

Empiricism belongs to epistemology, which is concerned with studying the nature, origins and boundaries of knowledge. Empiricists claim that knowledge of the world and its objects is derived from sensory experience and empirical evidence, and can only be known and justified through experience. Concepts based on reason, and intuitive propositions that can be either true or false, are rejected as unreliable since they are not based on observational evidence.

Finnis' 7 basic goods

Finnis has outlined seven basic goods, which motivate all human endeavour and are fundamental to all human life. They are not listed hierarchically nor do they derive from other goods and are irreducible to other things. The first three are substantive, which means they exist prior to action, and the remaining four are reflexive, which means they depend on the choices we make.

Finnis' 9 basic requirements of practical reasonableness

There are nine methodological requirements of practical reasonableness, which are claimed by Finnis to enable us to make decisions about how to act, what basic goods to choose and generally how to order our lives. They are also purported to be fundamental to the concept of natural law.

Formalism

There are various degrees and types of formalism. However, in general, legal formalists express the view that judges and other public institutions should confine their deliberations to interpreting legal texts, such as statute and case law, which describe what the law *is*. They hold that judges should constrain any tendency towards activism, simply apply the appropriate legal rule and refrain from interpreting what they believe the law *ought* to be, ignoring social interests and public policy, for example.

GLOSSARY OF TERMS

Fuller's inner morality of law	Fuller offers eight key measures to ensure that law-making adheres to a minimum standard. If a law exhibits all aspects, it is then considered to be good (or moral) law.
Hart's central tenets of legal positivism	H.L.A. Hart attempts to provide a classification of main themes that are characteristic of legal positivism, set out in his 1983 *Essays in Jurisprudence and Philosophy*:

- laws are commands of human beings;
- there is no necessary connection between law and morals, or law as it is and law as it ought to be;
- the analysis of legal concepts is worth pursuing and is to be distinguished from historical enquiries, from sociological inquiries and from the criticism or appraisal of law;
- a legal system is a closed legal system in which correct legal decisions can be deduced by logical means from predetermined legal rules;
- moral judgements cannot be established or defended, as statements of fact can, by rational argument, evidence or proof.

Hart's 'core' and 'penumbra'	For Hart, legal rules are not always certain; they possess both a core and a penumbra. This means all legal rules are established according to words that express a core meaning, and in penumbral cases there is some uncertainty as to the precise meaning of the words.
Hart's separability thesis	In his 1957 article, 'Positivism and the Separation of Law and Morals', Hart states, 'there is no necessary connection between law and morals or law as it is and ought to be'. This is not the same as saying that law and morals are automatically separate, nor is he arguing for a strict separation between law and morals. Hart's thesis simply promotes moral neutrality, in that general jurisprudence must not be committed in advance to conclusions about the moral value of law.
Indeterminacy of the law	The idea of the logical indeterminacy of law refers to the belief that legal rules are so indeterminate that they fail to impose any meaningful constraint on judicial decision-making. In other words, there is no reliably unambiguous right answer for any legal problem until determined by statute or legal judgment.
Jurisprudence	Jurisprudence is described as the philosophy or theory of law. Historically, it derives from the Latin term *juris prudentia*, which means the study, knowledge or science of the law.

Kant's categorical moral imperative	Kant's categorical moral imperative comprises three important principles; the latter principle combines the first two:

- *Universal law formulation*: An individual has a duty to act only on moral rules that he would be willing to impose on anyone else; therefore moral acts of obligation must be capable of universal application (without contradiction).

- *Humanity or end-in-itself formulation*: Always treat others as ends and not means; to treat other people as ends requires respecting each person as an autonomous rational moral agent with their own aspirations, goals and projects.

- *Kingdom-of-ends formulation*: Every rational being must so act as if he were, through his maxim, always a legislating member in the universal kingdom of ends.

Karl Llewellyn's 'law jobs'	Llewellyn referred to the basic functions of law as 'law jobs', with the aim of using this relatively simple theoretical framework to analyse and assess the legal institution's contribution to, and achievements within, society – relating to, for example, justice, efficacy and the greater good of all members of society.
Legal discourse	Legal discourse refers to law's language (as text and speech) as a distinctive communicative form that has both a prescriptive and normative character. It indicates the specific contexts and relationships implicated in, for example, the hierarchical and historically produced uses of language. Legal discourse is commonly analysed from within the context of, for example, legal theory, philosophy, semiotics and formal logic.
Legal fictions	When a legal rule or principle is grounded on a false or inaccurate premise, we refer to this as a legal fiction. For example, the vicarious liability rule finds an employer at fault and responsible for the actions of their employees, irrespective of any personal involvement.
Legal semiotics	The term legal semiotics relates to the study of law's language in constituting a particular environment of signs, symbols, meanings and rhetorical forms.
Libertarianism	Libertarianism, or 'entitlement theory', understands justice to be a purely historical issue in that, as Robert Nozick has stated, 'whether a distribution is just depends on how it came about'.
Marxian false consciousness	The reality of production relations means a manufacturer or employer is always in a favourable position. The law as a 'mirror of inequalities in society' represents a dominant world class view, in which, although tradition is an important factor, material and economic forces will always determine the evolution and content of laws.

GLOSSARY OF TERMS

Metaphysics

Metaphysics originates from the Greek words, indicating 'beyond' and 'physics', so what comes after appearance, or is outside (beyond) objective experience. It is a branch of philosophy that deals with the difficult questions of 'being' and 'the world', space and time, cause and effect, and so addresses first principles such as: what is the nature of reality and how can we know or experience the world? A metaphysical approach to a legal problem would be: how is it possible to know the truth of legal content and what makes legal content true?

Normative jurisprudence

The starting point of normative jurisprudence is the already established concept of law and so, having understood what the law *is*, it aims to understand the moral basis for the law. In other words, it is concerned with what the law *ought* to be. It seeks to provide a theory that determines what is morally right and just and is, therefore, concerned about the criteria by which the law should be evaluated.

Procedural justice

Procedural justice is concerned with the idea of the principle of fairness in relation to the mechanisms and processes that facilitate the allocation of goods and resources, as well as the fairness of dispute resolution processes – as opposed to the mere fact of equal distribution.

Rawls' original position

Rawls envisages a hypothetical original position from which rational human beings are able to decide which conditions are favourable to impose on people and organise a just society. This is achieved by social cooperation, in which people imagine themselves as free and equal, and then jointly agree upon and commit themselves to determining the principles of social and political justice.

Rawls' veil of ignorance

Behind the veil of ignorance any knowledge of individual distinguishing features is excluded. It ensures impartiality as people are unaware of status, class, race, natural ability, privilege or wealth; therefore, 'justice as fairness' is assured along with a unanimous result because everyone's interests are uniformly reconciled. All decisions made in this way would be authoritative and binding.

Semiotics

Semiotics refers to the role of linguistic signs in social life and how they are able to generate meaning and precede language. In semiotic analysis, for example, a plate of food is no longer simply steak and kidney pie, chips and apple crumble, rather it comprises a sign system that signifies matters of taste, status, class, sophistication and ethnicity.

The semantic sting

The semantic sting refers to the argument that there can only be a debate on 'what law is' if law-makers share and are in agreement on factual criteria about the grounds of law, the appropriate content and validity of legal rules. For Dworkin this represents a rather simplistic view of the relationship between law and language because even the word 'law' is an interpretative concept and depends on certain specific criteria. Dworkin's semantic sting argument claims that Hart's concept cannot explain what makes a statement of law true or false, and (wrongly) assumes any real disagreement about the law is impossible.

The sociological perspective

The sociological perspective contains three important principles. (1) The way in which society is structured, social organisation, comprises a range of institutions: cultural, political, economic and legal. (2) Social stratification means these institutions interact with and influence each other on a number of levels. This often produces disagreement that can result in, for example, forms of discrimination and class conflict. (3) Such institutions and clusters may be analysed in terms of their specific social function – for example, the role of the state in relation to press freedom v. privacy.

Utilitarianism

Utilitarianism is identified with the writing of Jeremy Bentham and J.S. Mill, and determines that the moral worth of an action, rule or principle can only be judged by its outcome. The individual as a distinct entity is ignored in favour of prioritising the promotion of collective human welfare, namely 'the greatest good for the greatest number'.

▉ Other useful terms

Absolutism

A belief in absolute principles relating to political, philosophical, ethical or theological matters. So, moral absolutism refers to the ethical view that certain actions are absolutely right or wrong, irrespective of other circumstances such as their consequences or the intentions behind them.

Dialectic

The art of arriving at the truth via the exchange of logical arguments. This process is associated with Hegel, whose critical method of arriving at the truth consisted of stating a thesis, developing a contradictory antithesis and combining and resolving them into a coherent synthesis.

GLOSSARY OF TERMS

Epistemology

Refers to the theory of knowledge, in particular its methods, validity and scope; for example, how do we know, what are the necessary and sufficient conditions of knowledge and what are its sources, structure and limits?

Essentialism

The essentialist view on gender, sexuality, race, ethnicity, or other group characteristics is that they are fixed traits, which ignores variation among group members as secondary. In relation to feminist legal discourse, essentialism describes how women are reduced to a universal property which dismisses their individuality and diversity.

Metanarrative (or meta-narrative)

Metanarratives are the story beyond the story: stories that are over-arching, all-encompassing explanations of historical meaning, experience or knowledge. They have been referred to (negatively) in critical theory, and particularly postmodernism, as totalising – in that they place all reality within a common framework.

Methodology

A particular method or set of procedures used by a discipline.

Moral realism

The idea that moral truth or moral facts are grounded in the nature of things and in this sense they are 'real'. It follows that it is possible to discover (not decide) what these moral facts are. Moral judgements can, therefore, be objectively true or false rather than simply produced by subjective and variable human reactions and attitudes.

Moral relativism

The belief that right and wrong are not absolute values, on the basis that different individuals or cultures have different moral standards. Moral standards or moral judgements are, therefore, personalised according to individual circumstances or cultural orientation.

Normative ethics

Refers to that part of moral philosophy, or ethics, concerned with advancing criteria with which to distinguish what is morally right and wrong.

Ontology

Ontology belongs to the branch of metaphysics that deals with the nature of being and the essence of things. An ontology of law might focus on legal rules, sources of law or methods of judicial reasoning in order to explain law's function in the social world.

Phenomenology

Phenomenology refers to the study of the structure of phenomena, of things such as experience or consciousness. It is a philosophy or method of inquiry (following the continental tradition, exemplified by Heidegger, Husserl and Hegel) based on the premise that reality consists of objects and events as they are perceived or understood in human consciousness and not of anything independent of human consciousness.

Postmodernism	Postmodernism is largely a modern multi-disciplinary reaction to the assumed certainty of scientific, or objective, truths that purport to explain everything. It is post because it denies the existence of any ultimate principles or objective human knowledge acquired through reason.
Rationalism	The idea that reason, rather than sensory experience, is central to our understanding of the world, and the foundation of certainty in knowledge.
Reductionism	An attempt or tendency to explain a complex set of facts, entities, phenomena, structures or statements by another, simpler set.
Reification	The treatment of something abstract or someone as if they were an object. Reification, in Marxist legal theory, describes the process of using human beings as commodities or things.
Relativism	The doctrine that knowledge, truth and morality exist only in relation to culture, society or historical context, and are not absolute.
Scepticism	A persistent doubt as to the authenticity of accepted beliefs or knowledge.
Subjectivism	The view that moral judgement, for example, is dependent on individual, personal and arbitrary beliefs rather than on rational and objective standards.
Syllogism	A form of deductive reasoning in which a conclusion is drawn from two given or assumed propositions (premises). For example, all humans need food, sleep and shelter (the major premise), I am a human (the minor premise), therefore I need food, sleep and shelter (the conclusion).
Teleology	The explanation of phenomena by the ultimate purpose they serve (consequences) rather than by postulated causes.

Index